MW00604499

PERT Math

Workbook

2022

A Comprehensive Review

+ 2 Full Length PERT Math

Practice Tests

By

Reza Nazari

Copyright © 2022
Effortless Math Education Inc.

All rights reserved. No part of this publication may be reproduced, stored in a retrieval system, or transmitted in any form or by any means, electronic, mechanical, photocopying, recording, scanning, or otherwise, except as permitted under Section 107 or 108 of the 1976 United States Copyright Ac, without permission of the author.

Effortless Math provides unofficial test prep products for a variety of tests and exams. It is not affiliated with or endorsed by any official organizations.

All inquiries should be addressed to:
info@effortlessMath.com
www.EffortlessMath.com

ISBN: 978-1-63719-240-5

Published by: **Effortless Math Education Inc.**

For Online Math Practice Visit www.EffortlessMath.com

Welcome to
PERT Math Prep
2022

Thank you for choosing Effortless Math for your PERT Math test preparation and congratulations on making the decision to take the PERT test! It's a remarkable move you are taking, one that shouldn't be diminished in any capacity.

That's why you need to use every tool possible to ensure you succeed on the test with the highest possible score, and this extensive math workbook is one such tool.

If math has never been a strong subject for you, don't worry! This book along with our online PERT Math resources will help you prepare for (and even ACE) the PERT Math test. As test day draws nearer, effective preparation becomes increasingly more important. Thankfully, you have this comprehensive workbook to help you get ready for the test. With this book and Effortless Math online resources, you can feel confident that you will be more than ready for the PERT Math test when the time comes.

First and foremost, it is important to note that this book is a workbook and not a textbook. Every lesson of this practice book was carefully developed to ensure that you are making the most effective use of your time while preparing for the test. This up-to-date book reflects the 2022 test guidelines and will put you on the right track to hone your math skills, overcome exam anxiety, and boost your confidence, so that you can have your best to succeed on the PERT Math test.

This exercise book will:

☑ Explain the format of the PERT Math test.

☑ Describe specific test-taking strategies that you can use on the test.

☑ Provide PERT Math test-taking tips.

☑ Help you identify the areas in which you need to concentrate your study time.

☑ Offer exercises that help you develop the basic math skills you will learn in each section.

☑ Give **2 realistic and full-length practice tests** (featuring new question types) with detailed answers to help you measure your exam readiness and build confidence.

This resource contains comprehensive practice questions and exercises that you will need to prepare for the PERT Math test. You'll get numerous skill building exercises as well as tips and techniques on how to prepare for your PERT math test.

In addition, in the following pages you'll find:

➢ **How to Use This Book Effectively** – This section provides you with step-by-step instructions on how to get the most out of this comprehensive study guide.

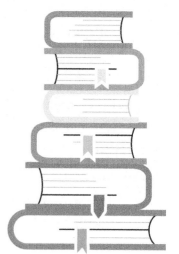

➢ **How to study for the PERT Math Test** – A six-step study program has been developed to help you make the best use of this book and prepare for your PERT Math test. Here you'll find tips and strategies to guide your study program and help you understand PERT Math and how to ace the test.

➤ **PERT Math Review** – Learn everything you need to know about the PERT Math test.

➤ **PERT Math Test-Taking Strategies** – Learn how to effectively put these recommended test-taking techniques into use for improving your PERT Math score.

➤ **Test Day Tips** – Review these tips to make sure you will do your best when the big day comes.

Effortless Math's PERT Online Center

Effortless Math Online PERT Center offers a complete study program, including the following:

✓ Step-by-step instructions on how to prepare for the PERT Math test

✓ Numerous PERT Math worksheets to help you measure your math skills

✓ Complete list of PERT Math formulas

✓ Video lessons for all PERT Math topics

✓ Full-length PERT Math practice tests

✓ And much more…

No Registration Required.

Visit **EffortlessMath.com/PERT** to find your online PERT Math resources.

How to Use This Book Effectively

Look no further when you need a study program to improve your math skills to succeed on the math portion of the PERT test. Each chapter of this comprehensive workbook will provide you with the knowledge, tools, and understanding needed for every topic covered on the test.

It's imperative that you understand each topic before moving onto another one, as that's the way to guarantee your success. You can use Effortless Math online course (a free course) to find examples and a step-by-step guide of every math concept in this workbook to better understand the content that will be on the test. To get the best possible results from this book:

- ➢ **Begin studying long before your test date**. This provides you ample time to learn the different math concepts. The earlier you begin studying for the test, the sharper your skills will be. Do not procrastinate! Provide yourself with plenty of time to learn the concepts and feel comfortable that you understand them when your test date arrives.

- ➢ **Practice consistently**. Study PERT Math concepts at least 20 to 30 minutes a day. Remember, slow and steady wins the race, which can be applied to preparing for the PERT Math test. Instead of cramming to tackle everything at once, be patient and learn the math topics in short bursts.

- ➢ Whenever you get a math problem wrong, **mark it off, and review it later** to make sure you understand the concept.

- ➢ Start each session by **looking over the previous material.**

- ➢ Once you've reviewed the book's exercises, **take a practice test at the back of the book** to gauge your level of readiness. Then, review your results. Read detailed answers and solutions for each question you missed.

- ➢ **Take another practice test** to get an idea of how ready you are to take the actual exam. Taking the practice tests will give you the confidence you need on test day. Simulate the PERT testing environment by sitting in a quiet room free from distraction. Make sure to clock yourself with a timer.

How to Study for the PERT Math Test

Studying for the PERT Math test can be a really daunting and boring task. What's the best way to go about it? Is there a certain study method that works better than others? Well, studying for the PERT Math can be done effectively. The following six-step program has been designed to make preparing for the PERT Math test more efficient and less overwhelming.

Step 1 - Create a study plan
Step 2 - Choose your study resources
Step 3 - Review, Learn, Practice
Step 4 - Learn and practice test-taking strategies
Step 5 - Learn the PERT Test format and take practice tests
Step 6 - Analyze your performance

STEP 1: Create a Study Plan

It's always easier to get things done when you have a plan. Creating a study plan for the PERT Math test can help you to stay on track with your studies. It's important to sit down and prepare a study plan with what works with your life, work, and any other obligations you may have. Devote enough time each day to studying. It's also a great 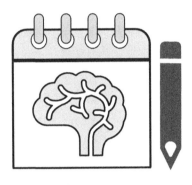 idea to break down each section of the exam into blocks and study one concept at a time.

It's important to understand that there is no "right" way to create a study plan. Your study plan will be personalized based on your specific needs and learning style.

Follow these guidelines to create an effective study plan for your PERT Math test:

★ **Analyze your learning style and study habits** – Everyone has a different learning style. It is essential to embrace your individuality and the unique way you learn. Think about what works and what doesn't work for you. Do you prefer PERT Math prep books or a combination of textbooks and video lessons? Does it work better for you if you study every night for thirty minutes or is it more effective to study in the morning before going to work?

★ **Evaluate your schedule** – Review your current schedule and find out how much time you can consistently devote to PERT Math study.

★ **Develop a schedule** – Now it's time to add your study schedule to your calendar like any other obligation. Schedule time for study, practice, and review. Plan out which topic you will study on which day to ensure that you're devoting enough time to each concept. Develop a study plan that is mindful, realistic, and flexible.

★ **Stick to your schedule** – A study plan is only effective when it is followed consistently. You should try to develop a study plan that you can follow for the length of your study program.

★ **Evaluate your study plan and adjust as needed** – Sometimes you need to adjust your plan when you have new commitments. Check in with yourself regularly to make sure that you're not falling behind in your study plan. Remember, the most important thing is sticking to your plan. Your study plan is all about helping you be more productive. If you find that your study plan is not as effective as you want, don't get discouraged. It's okay to make changes as you figure out what works best for you.

STEP 2: Choose Your Study Resources

There are numerous textbooks and online resources available for the PERT Math test, and it may not be clear where to begin. Don't worry! This exercise book reviews all PERT Math concepts and topics. In addition to the book content, you can also use Effortless Math's online resources. (video lessons, worksheets, formulas, etc.) On each page, there is a link (and

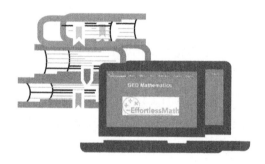

a QR code) to an online webpage which provides a comprehensive review of the topic, step-by-step instruction, video tutorial, and numerous examples and exercises to help you fully understand the concept.

Simply visit EffortlessMath.com/PERT to find your online PERT Math resources.

STEP 3: Review, Learn, Practice

This PERT Math exercise book breaks down each subject into specific skills or content areas. For instance, the percent concept is separated into different topics–percent calculation, percent increase and decrease, percent problems, etc. Use this book to help you go over all key math concepts and topics on the PERT Math test.

As you review each topic, take notes or highlight the concepts you would like to go over again in the future. If you're unfamiliar with a topic or something is difficult for you, use the link (or the QR code) at the top of the page to find the webpage that provides more instruction about that topic. For each math topic, plenty of instructions, step-by-step guides, and examples are provided to ensure you get a good grasp of the material.

Quickly review the topics you do understand to get a brush-up of the material. Be sure to do the practice questions provided at the end of every chapter to measure your understanding of the concepts.

STEP 4: Learn and Practice Test-taking Strategies

In the following sections, you will find important test-taking strategies and tips that can help you earn extra points. You'll learn how to think strategically and when to guess if you don't know the answer to a question. Using PERT Math test-taking strategies and tips can help you raise your score and do well on the test. Apply test taking strategies on the practice tests to help you boost your confidence.

STEP 5: **Learn the PERT Test Format and Take Practice Tests**

The PERT *Test Review* section provides information about the structure of the PERT test. Read this section to learn more about the PERT test structure, different test sections, the number of questions in each section, and the section time limits. When you have a prior understanding of the test format and different types of PERT Math questions, you'll feel more confident when you take the actual exam.

Once you have read through the instructions and lessons and feel like you are ready to go – take advantage of both of the full-length PERT Math practice tests available in this exercise book. Use the practice tests to sharpen your skills and build confidence.

The PERT Math practice tests offered at the end of the book are formatted similarly to the actual PERT Math test. When you take each practice test, try to simulate actual testing conditions. To take the practice tests, sit in a quiet space, time yourself, and work through as many of the questions as time allows. The practice tests are followed by detailed answer explanations to help you find your weak areas, learn from your mistakes, and raise your PERT Math score.

STEP 6: **Analyze Your Performance**

After taking the practice tests, look over the answer keys and explanations to learn which questions you answered correctly and which you did not. Never be discouraged if you make a few mistakes. See them as a learning opportunity. This will highlight your strengths and weaknesses.

You can use the results to determine if you need additional practice or if you are ready to take the actual PERT Math test.

Looking for more?

Visit EffortlessMath.com/PERT to find hundreds of PERT Math worksheets, video tutorials, practice tests, PERT Math formulas, and much more.

Or scan this QR code.

No Registration Required.

PERT Test Review

The Postsecondary Education Readiness Test, is known as the PERT, is a test to determine the appropriate level of college course work for an incoming student. In essence, it is a broad and quick assessment of students' academic abilities. The PERT test consists of three multiple-choice separate exams:

- Mathematics
- Reading
- Writing

The PERT test is a Computer Adaptive Test (CAT). It means that if the correct answer is chosen, the next question will be harder. If the answer given is incorrect, the next question will be easier. This also means that once an answer is selected on the CAT it cannot be changed.

The mathematics portion of the PERT test contains 30 multiple-choice questions. The test covers data analysis, geometry, and algebra on both intermediate and basic levels. The topics on the math test includes:

- linear equations, linear inequalities, literal equation, and quadratic formulas
- simultaneous linear equations with two variables
- evaluating algebraic expressions
- translating between lines and inspecting equations on coordinate planes
- dividing by binomials and monomials
- adding, subtracting, multiplying, dividing, simplifying and factoring polynomial

Students are not allowed to use calculator when taking a PERT assessment. A pop-up calculator is embedded in the test for some questions. Scores on the PERT test range from 50 to 150. On the PERT mathematics exam, you will be placed in lower-level developmental education if you score between 50-95. If your score is between 96 and 113, then you will be placed in higher level developmental education. A score of 114 to 122 will enable you to be place in Intermediate Algebra (MAT 1033). Score of 123 or higher will allow you to take College Algebra or higher (MAC 1105).

PERT Math Test-Taking Strategies

Here are some test-taking strategies that you can use to maximize your performance and results on the PERT Math test.

#1: USE THIS APPROACH TO ANSWER EVERY PERT MATH QUESTION

- Review the question to identify keywords and important information.
- Translate the keywords into math operations so you can solve the problem.
- Review the answer choices. What are the differences between answer choices?
- Draw or label a diagram if needed.
- Try to find patterns.
- Find the right method to answer the question. Use straightforward math, plug in numbers, or test the answer choices (backsolving).
- Double-check your work.

#2: USE EDUCATED GUESSING

This approach is applicable to the problems you understand to some degree but cannot solve using straightforward math. In such cases, try to filter out as many answer choices as possible before picking an answer. In cases where you don't have a clue about what a certain problem entails, don't waste any time trying to eliminate answer choices. Just choose one randomly before moving onto the next question.

As you can ascertain, direct solutions are the most optimal approach. Carefully read through the question, determine what the solution is using the math you have learned before, then coordinate the answer with one of the choices available to you. Are you stumped? Make your best guess, then move on.

Don't leave any fields empty! Even if you're unable to work out a problem, strive to answer it. Take a guess if you have to. You will not lose points by getting an answer wrong, though you may gain a point by getting it correct!

#3: BALLPARK

A ballpark answer is a rough approximation. When we become overwhelmed by calculations and figures, we end up making silly mistakes. A decimal that is moved by one unit can change an answer from right to wrong, regardless of the number of steps that you went through to get it. That's where ballparking can play a big part.

If you think you know what the correct answer may be (even if it's just a ballpark answer), you'll usually have the ability to eliminate a couple of choices. While answer choices are usually based on the average student error and/or values that are closely tied, you will still be able to weed out choices that are way far afield. Try to find answers that aren't in the proverbial ballpark when you're looking for a wrong answer on a multiple-choice question. This is an optimal approach to eliminating answers to a problem.

#4 : BACKSOLVING

A majority of questions on the PERT Math test will be in multiple-choice format. Many test-takers prefer multiple-choice questions, as at least the answer is right there. You'll typically have four answers to pick from. You simply need to figure out which one is correct. Usually, the best way to go about doing so is "backsolving."

As mentioned earlier, direct solutions are the most optimal approach to answering a question. Carefully read through a problem, calculate a solution, then correspond the answer with one of the choices displayed in front of you. If you can't calculate a solution, your next best approach involves "backsolving."

When backsolving a problem, contrast one of your answer options against the problem you are asked, then see which of them is most relevant. More often than not, answer choices are listed in ascending or descending order. In such cases, try out the choices B or C. If it's not correct, you can go either down or up from there.

#5 : PLUGGING IN NUMBERS

"Plugging in numbers" is a strategy that can be applied to a wide range of different math problems on the PERT Math test. This approach is typically used to simplify a challenging question so that it is more understandable. By using the strategy carefully, you can find the answer without too much trouble.

The concept is fairly straightforward–replace unknown variables in a problem with certain values. When selecting a number, consider the following:

- Choose a number that's basic (just not too basic). Generally, you should avoid choosing 1 (or even 0). A decent choice is 2.

- Try not to choose a number that is displayed in the problem.

- Make sure you keep your numbers different if you need to choose at least two of them.

- More often than not, choosing numbers merely lets you filter out some of your answer choices. As such, don't just go with the first choice that gives you the right answer.

- If several answers seem correct, then you'll need to choose another value and try again. This time, though, you'll just need to check choices that haven't been eliminated yet.

- If your question contains fractions, then a potential right answer may involve either an LCD (least common denominator) or an LCD multiple.

- 100 is the number you should choose when you are dealing with problems involving percentages.

PERT Math – Test Day Tips

After practicing and reviewing all the math concepts you've been taught, and taking some PERT mathematics practice tests, you'll be prepared for test day. Consider the following tips to be extra-ready come test time.

Before Your Test

What to do the night before:

- **Relax!** One day before your test, study lightly or skip studying altogether. You shouldn't attempt to learn something new, either. There are plenty of reasons why studying the evening before a big test can work against you. Put it this way— a marathoner wouldn't go out for a sprint before the day of a big race. Mental marathoners—such as yourself—should not study for any more than one hour 24 hours before a PERT test. That's because your brain requires some rest to be at its best. The night before your exam, spend some time with family or friends, or read a book.

- **Avoid bright screens** - You'll have to get some good shuteye the night before your test. Bright screens (such as the ones coming from your laptop, TV, or mobile device) should be avoided altogether. Staring at such a screen will keep your brain up, making it hard to drift asleep at a reasonable hour.

- **Make sure your dinner is healthy** - The meal that you have for dinner should be nutritious. Be sure to drink plenty of water as well. Load up on your complex carbohydrates, much like a marathon runner would do. Pasta, rice, and potatoes are ideal options here, as are vegetables and protein sources.

- **Get your bag ready for test day** - The night prior to your test, pack your bag with your stationery, admissions pass, ID, and any other gear that you need. Keep the bag right by your front door.

- **Make plans to reach the testing site** - Before going to sleep, ensure that you understand precisely how you will arrive at the site of the test. If parking is something you'll have to find first, plan for it. If you're dependent on public transit, then review the schedule. You should also make sure that the train/bus/subway/streetcar you use will be running. Find out about road closures as well. If a parent or friend is accompanying you, ensure that they understand what steps they have to take as well.

The Day of the Test

- **Get up reasonably early, but not too early.**

- **Have breakfast** - Breakfast improves your concentration, memory, and mood. As such, make sure the breakfast that you eat in the morning is healthy. The last thing you want to be is distracted by a grumbling tummy. If it's not your own stomach making those noises, another test taker close to you might be instead. Prevent discomfort or embarrassment by consuming a healthy breakfast. Bring a snack with you if you think you'll need it.

- **Follow your daily routine** - Do you watch Good Morning America each morning while getting ready for the day? Don't break your usual habits on the day of the test. Likewise, if coffee isn't something you drink in the morning, then don't take up the habit hours before your test. Routine consistency lets you concentrate on the main objective–doing the best you can on your test.

- **Wear layers** - Dress yourself up in comfortable layers. You should be ready for any kind of internal temperature. If it gets too warm during the test, take a layer off.

- **Get there on time** - The last thing you want to do is get to the test site late. Rather, you should be there 45 minutes prior to the start of the test. Upon your arrival, try not to hang out with anybody who is nervous. Any anxious energy they exhibit shouldn't influence you.

- **Leave the books at home** - No books should be brought to the test site. If you start developing anxiety before the test, books could encourage you to do some last-minute studying, which will only hinder you. Keep the books far away–better yet, leave them at home.

- **Make your voice heard** - If something is off, speak to a proctor. If medical attention is needed or if you'll require anything, consult the proctor prior to the start of the test. Any doubts you have should be clarified. You should be entering the test site with a state of mind that is completely clear.

- **Have faith in yourself** - When you feel confident, you will be able to perform at your best. When you are waiting for the test to begin, envision yourself receiving an outstanding result. Try to see yourself as someone who knows all the answers, no matter what the questions are. A lot of athletes tend to use this technique–particularly before a big competition. Your expectations will be reflected by your performance.

During your test

■ **Be calm and breathe deeply** - You need to relax before the test, and some deep breathing will go a long way to help you do that. Be confident and calm. You got this. Everybody feels a little stressed out just before an evaluation of any kind is set to begin. Learn some effective breathing exercises. Spend a minute meditating before the test starts. Filter out any negative thoughts you have. Exhibit confidence when having such thoughts.

■ **Concentrate on the test** - Refrain from comparing yourself to anyone else. You shouldn't be distracted by the people near you or random noise. Concentrate exclusively on the test. If you find yourself irritated by surrounding noises, earplugs can be used to block sounds off close to you. Don't forget—the test is going to last several hours if you're taking more than one subject of the test. Some of that time will be dedicated to brief sections. Concentrate on the specific section you are working on during a particular moment. Do not let your mind wander off to upcoming or previous sections.

■ **Try to answer each question individually** - Focus only on the question you are working on. Use one of the test-taking strategies to solve the problem. If you aren't able to come up with an answer, don't get frustrated. Simply skip that question, then move onto the next one.

■ **Don't forget to breathe!** Whenever you notice your mind wandering, your stress levels boosting, or frustration brewing, take a thirty-second break. Shut your eyes, drop your pencil, breathe deeply, and let your shoulders relax. You will end up being more productive when you allow yourself to relax for a moment.

■ **Optimize your breaks** - When break time comes, use the restroom, have a snack, and reactivate your energy for the subsequent section. Doing some stretches can help stimulate your blood flow.

After your test

■ **Take it easy** - You will need to set some time aside to relax and decompress once the test has concluded. There is no need to stress yourself out about what you could've said, or what you may have done wrong. At this point, there's nothing you can do about it. Your energy and time would be better spent on something that will bring you happiness for the remainder of your day.

■ **Redoing the test** - Did you pass the test? Congratulations! Your hard work paid off!

If you have failed your test, though, don't worry! The test can be retaken. In such cases, you will need to follow the retake policy. You also need to re-register to take the exam again.

Contents

Simplifying Fractions

✏️ *Simplify each fraction.*

1) $\frac{10}{15} =$

2) $\frac{8}{20} =$

3) $\frac{12}{42} =$

4) $\frac{5}{20} =$

5) $\frac{6}{18} =$

6) $\frac{18}{27} =$

7) $\frac{15}{55} =$

8) $\frac{24}{54} =$

9) $\frac{63}{72} =$

10) $\frac{40}{64} =$

11) $\frac{23}{46} =$

12) $\frac{35}{63} =$

13) $\frac{32}{36} =$

14) $\frac{81}{99} =$

15) $\frac{16}{64} =$

16) $\frac{14}{35} =$

17) $\frac{19}{38} =$

18) $\frac{18}{54} =$

19) $\frac{56}{70} =$

20) $\frac{40}{45} =$

21) $\frac{9}{90} =$

22) $\frac{20}{25} =$

23) $\frac{32}{48} =$

24) $\frac{7}{49} =$

25) $\frac{18}{48} =$

26) $\frac{54}{108} =$

bit.ly/3HtzOqy
Find more at

Simplifying Fractions - Answers

✑ **Simplify each fraction.**

1) $\dfrac{10}{15} = \dfrac{2}{3}$

2) $\dfrac{8}{20} = \dfrac{2}{5}$

3) $\dfrac{12}{42} = \dfrac{2}{7}$

4) $\dfrac{5}{20} = \dfrac{1}{4}$

5) $\dfrac{6}{18} = \dfrac{1}{3}$

6) $\dfrac{18}{27} = \dfrac{2}{3}$

7) $\dfrac{15}{55} = \dfrac{3}{11}$

8) $\dfrac{24}{54} = \dfrac{4}{9}$

9) $\dfrac{63}{72} = \dfrac{7}{8}$

10) $\dfrac{40}{64} = \dfrac{5}{8}$

11) $\dfrac{23}{46} = \dfrac{1}{2}$

12) $\dfrac{35}{63} = \dfrac{5}{9}$

13) $\dfrac{32}{36} = \dfrac{8}{9}$

14) $\dfrac{81}{99} = \dfrac{9}{11}$

15) $\dfrac{16}{64} = \dfrac{1}{4}$

16) $\dfrac{14}{35} = \dfrac{2}{5}$

17) $\dfrac{19}{38} = \dfrac{1}{2}$

18) $\dfrac{18}{54} = \dfrac{1}{3}$

19) $\dfrac{56}{70} = \dfrac{4}{5}$

20) $\dfrac{40}{45} = \dfrac{8}{9}$

21) $\dfrac{9}{90} = \dfrac{1}{10}$

22) $\dfrac{20}{25} = \dfrac{4}{5}$

23) $\dfrac{32}{48} = \dfrac{2}{3}$

24) $\dfrac{7}{49} = \dfrac{1}{7}$

25) $\dfrac{18}{48} = \dfrac{3}{8}$

26) $\dfrac{54}{108} = \dfrac{1}{2}$

Adding and Subtracting Fractions

✎ *Calculate and write the answer in lowest term.*

1) $\frac{1}{5} + \frac{1}{7} =$

2) $\frac{3}{7} + \frac{4}{5} =$

3) $\frac{3}{8} - \frac{1}{9} =$

4) $\frac{4}{5} - \frac{5}{9} =$

5) $\frac{2}{9} + \frac{1}{3} =$

6) $\frac{3}{10} + \frac{2}{5} =$

7) $\frac{9}{10} - \frac{4}{5} =$

8) $\frac{7}{9} - \frac{3}{7} =$

9) $\frac{3}{4} + \frac{1}{3} =$

10) $\frac{3}{8} + \frac{2}{5} =$

11) $\frac{3}{4} - \frac{2}{5} =$

12) $\frac{7}{9} - \frac{2}{3} =$

13) $\frac{4}{9} + \frac{5}{6} =$

14) $\frac{2}{3} + \frac{1}{4} =$

15) $\frac{9}{10} - \frac{3}{5} =$

16) $\frac{7}{12} - \frac{1}{2} =$

17) $\frac{4}{5} + \frac{2}{3} =$

18) $\frac{5}{7} + \frac{1}{5} =$

19) $\frac{5}{9} - \frac{2}{5} =$

20) $\frac{3}{5} - \frac{2}{9} =$

21) $\frac{7}{9} + \frac{1}{7} =$

22) $\frac{5}{8} + \frac{2}{3} =$

23) $\frac{4}{7} + \frac{2}{3} =$

24) $\frac{6}{7} - \frac{4}{9} =$

25) $\frac{4}{5} - \frac{2}{15} =$

26) $\frac{2}{9} + \frac{4}{5} =$

bit.ly/3qIeMh5

Find more at

Adding and Subtracting Fractions - Answers

✎ *Calculate and write the answer in lowest term.*

1) $\frac{1}{5} + \frac{1}{7} = \frac{12}{35}$

2) $\frac{3}{7} + \frac{4}{5} = \frac{43}{35}$

3) $\frac{3}{8} - \frac{1}{9} = \frac{19}{72}$

4) $\frac{4}{5} - \frac{5}{9} = \frac{11}{45}$

5) $\frac{2}{9} + \frac{1}{3} = \frac{5}{9}$

6) $\frac{3}{10} + \frac{2}{5} = \frac{7}{10}$

7) $\frac{9}{10} - \frac{4}{5} = \frac{1}{10}$

8) $\frac{7}{9} - \frac{3}{7} = \frac{22}{63}$

9) $\frac{3}{4} + \frac{1}{3} = \frac{13}{12}$

10) $\frac{3}{8} + \frac{2}{5} = \frac{31}{40}$

11) $\frac{3}{4} - \frac{2}{5} = \frac{7}{20}$

12) $\frac{7}{9} - \frac{2}{3} = \frac{1}{9}$

13) $\frac{4}{9} + \frac{5}{6} = \frac{23}{18}$

14) $\frac{2}{3} + \frac{1}{4} = \frac{11}{12}$

15) $\frac{9}{10} - \frac{3}{5} = \frac{3}{10}$

16) $\frac{7}{12} - \frac{1}{2} = \frac{1}{12}$

17) $\frac{4}{5} + \frac{2}{3} = \frac{22}{15}$

18) $\frac{5}{7} + \frac{1}{5} = \frac{32}{35}$

19) $\frac{5}{9} - \frac{2}{5} = \frac{7}{45}$

20) $\frac{3}{5} - \frac{2}{9} = \frac{17}{45}$

21) $\frac{7}{9} + \frac{1}{7} = \frac{58}{63}$

22) $\frac{5}{8} + \frac{2}{3} = \frac{31}{24}$

23) $\frac{4}{7} + \frac{2}{3} = \frac{26}{21}$

24) $\frac{6}{7} - \frac{4}{9} = \frac{26}{63}$

25) $\frac{4}{5} - \frac{2}{15} = \frac{2}{3}$

26) $\frac{2}{9} + \frac{4}{5} = \frac{46}{45}$

Multiplying and Dividing Fractions

✍️ *Solve and write the answer in lowest term.*

1) $\frac{1}{2} \times \frac{4}{5} =$

2) $\frac{1}{5} \times \frac{6}{7} =$

3) $\frac{1}{3} \div \frac{1}{7} =$

4) $\frac{1}{7} \div \frac{3}{8} =$

5) $\frac{2}{3} \times \frac{4}{7} =$

6) $\frac{5}{7} \times \frac{3}{4} =$

7) $\frac{2}{5} \div \frac{3}{7} =$

8) $\frac{3}{7} \div \frac{5}{8} =$

9) $\frac{3}{8} \times \frac{4}{7} =$

10) $\frac{2}{9} \times \frac{6}{11} =$

11) $\frac{1}{10} \div \frac{3}{8} =$

12) $\frac{3}{10} \div \frac{4}{5} =$

13) $\frac{6}{7} \times \frac{4}{9} =$

14) $\frac{3}{7} \times \frac{5}{6} =$

15) $\frac{7}{9} \div \frac{6}{11} =$

16) $\frac{1}{15} \div \frac{2}{3} =$

17) $\frac{1}{13} \times \frac{1}{2} =$

18) $\frac{1}{12} \times \frac{4}{7} =$

19) $\frac{1}{15} \div \frac{4}{9} =$

20) $\frac{1}{16} \div \frac{1}{2} =$

21) $\frac{4}{7} \times \frac{5}{8} =$

22) $\frac{1}{11} \times \frac{4}{5} =$

23) $\frac{1}{18} \div \frac{5}{6} =$

24) $\frac{1}{15} \div \frac{3}{8} =$

25) $\frac{1}{11} \times \frac{3}{4} =$

26) $\frac{1}{14} \times \frac{2}{3} =$

Find more at bit.ly/3haSiQW

Multiplying and Dividing Fractions - Answers

✎ *Solve and write the answer in lowest term.*

1) $\frac{1}{2} \times \frac{4}{5} = \frac{2}{5}$

2) $\frac{1}{5} \times \frac{6}{7} = \frac{6}{35}$

3) $\frac{1}{3} \div \frac{1}{7} = \frac{7}{3}$

4) $\frac{1}{7} \div \frac{3}{8} = \frac{8}{21}$

5) $\frac{2}{3} \times \frac{4}{7} = \frac{8}{21}$

6) $\frac{5}{7} \times \frac{3}{4} = \frac{15}{28}$

7) $\frac{2}{5} \div \frac{3}{7} = \frac{14}{15}$

8) $\frac{3}{7} \div \frac{5}{8} = \frac{24}{35}$

9) $\frac{3}{8} \times \frac{4}{7} = \frac{3}{14}$

10) $\frac{2}{9} \times \frac{6}{11} = \frac{4}{33}$

11) $\frac{1}{10} \div \frac{3}{8} = \frac{4}{15}$

12) $\frac{3}{10} \div \frac{4}{5} = \frac{3}{8}$

13) $\frac{6}{7} \times \frac{4}{9} = \frac{8}{21}$

14) $\frac{3}{7} \times \frac{5}{6} = \frac{5}{14}$

15) $\frac{7}{9} \div \frac{6}{11} = \frac{77}{54}$

16) $\frac{1}{15} \div \frac{2}{3} = \frac{1}{10}$

17) $\frac{1}{13} \times \frac{1}{2} = \frac{1}{26}$

18) $\frac{1}{12} \times \frac{4}{7} = \frac{1}{21}$

19) $\frac{1}{15} \div \frac{4}{9} = \frac{3}{20}$

20) $\frac{1}{16} \div \frac{1}{2} = \frac{1}{8}$

21) $\frac{4}{7} \times \frac{5}{8} = \frac{5}{14}$

22) $\frac{1}{11} \times \frac{4}{5} = \frac{4}{55}$

23) $\frac{1}{18} \div \frac{5}{6} = \frac{1}{15}$

24) $\frac{1}{15} \div \frac{3}{8} = \frac{8}{45}$

25) $\frac{1}{11} \times \frac{3}{4} = \frac{3}{44}$

26) $\frac{1}{14} \times \frac{2}{3} = \frac{1}{21}$

Adding Mixed Numbers

✍ *Solve and write the answer in lowest terms.*

1) $3\frac{1}{5} + 2\frac{2}{9} =$

2) $1\frac{1}{7} + 5\frac{2}{5} =$

3) $4\frac{4}{5} + 1\frac{2}{7} =$

4) $2\frac{4}{7} + 2\frac{3}{5} =$

5) $1\frac{5}{6} + 1\frac{2}{5} =$

6) $3\frac{5}{7} + 1\frac{2}{9} =$

7) $3\frac{5}{8} + 2\frac{1}{3} =$

8) $1\frac{6}{7} + 3\frac{2}{9} =$

9) $2\frac{5}{9} + 1\frac{1}{4} =$

10) $3\frac{7}{9} + 2\frac{5}{6} =$

11) $2\frac{1}{10} + 2\frac{2}{5} =$

12) $1\frac{3}{10} + 3\frac{4}{5} =$

13) $3\frac{1}{12} + 2\frac{1}{3} =$

14) $5\frac{1}{11} + 1\frac{1}{2} =$

15) $3\frac{1}{21} + 2\frac{2}{3} =$

16) $4\frac{1}{24} + 1\frac{5}{8} =$

17) $2\frac{1}{25} + 3\frac{3}{5} =$

18) $3\frac{1}{15} + 2\frac{2}{10} =$

19) $5\frac{6}{7} + 2\frac{1}{3} =$

20) $2\frac{1}{8} + 3\frac{3}{4} =$

21) $2\frac{5}{7} + 2\frac{2}{21} =$

22) $4\frac{1}{6} + 1\frac{4}{5} =$

23) $3\frac{5}{6} + 1\frac{2}{7} =$

24) $2\frac{7}{8} + 3\frac{1}{3} =$

25) $3\frac{1}{17} + 1\frac{1}{2} =$

26) $1\frac{1}{18} + 1\frac{4}{9} =$

bit.ly/2M4oABB

Find more at

Adding Mixed Numbers - Answers

Solve and write the answer in lowest terms.

1) $3\frac{1}{5} + 2\frac{2}{9} = 5\frac{19}{45}$

2) $1\frac{1}{7} + 5\frac{2}{5} = 6\frac{19}{35}$

3) $4\frac{4}{5} + 1\frac{2}{7} = 6\frac{3}{35}$

4) $2\frac{4}{7} + 2\frac{3}{5} = 5\frac{6}{35}$

5) $1\frac{5}{6} + 1\frac{2}{5} = 3\frac{7}{30}$

6) $3\frac{5}{7} + 1\frac{2}{9} = 4\frac{59}{63}$

7) $3\frac{5}{8} + 2\frac{1}{3} = 5\frac{23}{24}$

8) $1\frac{6}{7} + 3\frac{2}{9} = 5\frac{5}{63}$

9) $2\frac{5}{9} + 1\frac{1}{4} = 3\frac{29}{36}$

10) $3\frac{7}{9} + 2\frac{5}{6} = 6\frac{11}{18}$

11) $2\frac{1}{10} + 2\frac{2}{5} = 4\frac{1}{2}$

12) $1\frac{3}{10} + 3\frac{4}{5} = 5\frac{1}{10}$

13) $3\frac{1}{12} + 2\frac{1}{3} = 5\frac{5}{12}$

14) $5\frac{1}{11} + 1\frac{1}{2} = 6\frac{13}{22}$

15) $3\frac{1}{21} + 2\frac{2}{3} = 5\frac{5}{7}$

16) $4\frac{1}{24} + 1\frac{5}{8} = 5\frac{2}{3}$

17) $2\frac{1}{25} + 3\frac{3}{5} = 5\frac{16}{25}$

18) $3\frac{1}{15} + 2\frac{2}{10} = 5\frac{4}{15}$

19) $5\frac{6}{7} + 2\frac{1}{3} = 8\frac{4}{21}$

20) $2\frac{1}{8} + 3\frac{3}{4} = 5\frac{7}{8}$

21) $2\frac{5}{7} + 2\frac{2}{21} = 4\frac{17}{21}$

22) $4\frac{1}{6} + 1\frac{4}{5} = 5\frac{29}{30}$

23) $3\frac{5}{6} + 1\frac{2}{7} = 5\frac{5}{42}$

24) $2\frac{7}{8} + 3\frac{1}{3} = 6\frac{5}{24}$

25) $3\frac{1}{17} + 1\frac{1}{2} = 4\frac{19}{34}$

26) $1\frac{1}{18} + 1\frac{4}{9} = 2\frac{1}{2}$

Subtracting Mixed Numbers

✍ *Solve and write the answer in lowest terms.*

1) $3\frac{2}{5} - 1\frac{2}{9} =$

2) $5\frac{3}{5} - 1\frac{1}{7} =$

3) $4\frac{2}{5} - 2\frac{2}{7} =$

4) $8\frac{3}{4} - 2\frac{1}{8} =$

5) $9\frac{5}{7} - 7\frac{4}{21} =$

6) $11\frac{7}{12} - 9\frac{5}{6} =$

7) $9\frac{5}{9} - 8\frac{1}{8} =$

8) $13\frac{7}{9} - 11\frac{3}{7} =$

9) $8\frac{7}{12} - 7\frac{3}{8} =$

10) $11\frac{5}{9} - 9\frac{1}{4} =$

11) $6\frac{5}{6} - 2\frac{2}{9} =$

12) $5\frac{7}{8} - 4\frac{1}{3} =$

13) $9\frac{5}{8} - 8\frac{1}{2} =$

14) $4\frac{9}{16} - 2\frac{1}{4} =$

15) $3\frac{2}{3} - 1\frac{2}{15} =$

16) $5\frac{1}{2} - 4\frac{2}{17} =$

17) $5\frac{6}{7} - 2\frac{1}{3} =$

18) $3\frac{3}{7} - 2\frac{2}{21} =$

19) $7\frac{3}{10} - 5\frac{2}{15} =$

20) $4\frac{5}{6} - 2\frac{2}{9} =$

21) $6\frac{3}{7} - 2\frac{2}{9} =$

22) $7\frac{4}{5} - 6\frac{3}{7} =$

23) $10\frac{2}{3} - 9\frac{5}{8} =$

24) $9\frac{3}{4} - 7\frac{4}{9} =$

25) $15\frac{4}{5} - 13\frac{12}{25} =$

26) $13\frac{5}{12} - 7\frac{5}{24} =$

bit.ly/3aD3KDG

Find more at

Subtracting Mixed Numbers - Answers

✏️ *Solve and write the answer in lowest terms.*

1) $3\frac{2}{5} - 1\frac{2}{9} = 2\frac{8}{45}$

2) $5\frac{3}{5} - 1\frac{1}{7} = 4\frac{16}{35}$

3) $4\frac{2}{5} - 2\frac{2}{7} = 2\frac{4}{35}$

4) $8\frac{3}{4} - 2\frac{1}{8} = 6\frac{5}{8}$

5) $9\frac{5}{7} - 7\frac{4}{21} = 2\frac{11}{21}$

6) $11\frac{7}{12} - 9\frac{5}{6} = 1\frac{3}{4}$

7) $9\frac{5}{9} - 8\frac{1}{8} = 1\frac{31}{72}$

8) $13\frac{7}{9} - 11\frac{3}{7} = 2\frac{22}{63}$

9) $8\frac{7}{12} - 7\frac{3}{8} = 1\frac{5}{24}$

10) $11\frac{5}{9} - 9\frac{1}{4} = 2\frac{11}{36}$

11) $6\frac{5}{6} - 2\frac{2}{9} = 4\frac{11}{18}$

12) $5\frac{7}{8} - 4\frac{1}{3} = 1\frac{13}{24}$

13) $9\frac{5}{8} - 8\frac{1}{2} = 1\frac{1}{8}$

14) $4\frac{9}{16} - 2\frac{1}{4} = 2\frac{5}{16}$

15) $3\frac{2}{3} - 1\frac{2}{15} = 2\frac{8}{15}$

16) $5\frac{1}{2} - 4\frac{2}{17} = 1\frac{13}{34}$

17) $5\frac{6}{7} - 2\frac{1}{3} = 3\frac{11}{21}$

18) $3\frac{3}{7} - 2\frac{2}{21} = 1\frac{1}{3}$

19) $7\frac{3}{10} - 5\frac{2}{15} = 2\frac{1}{6}$

20) $4\frac{5}{6} - 2\frac{2}{9} = 2\frac{11}{18}$

21) $6\frac{3}{7} - 2\frac{2}{9} = 4\frac{13}{63}$

22) $7\frac{4}{5} - 6\frac{3}{7} = 1\frac{13}{35}$

23) $10\frac{2}{3} - 9\frac{5}{8} = 1\frac{1}{24}$

24) $9\frac{3}{4} - 7\frac{4}{9} = 2\frac{11}{36}$

25) $15\frac{4}{5} - 13\frac{12}{25} = 2\frac{8}{25}$

26) $13\frac{5}{12} - 7\frac{5}{24} = 6\frac{5}{24}$

Multiplying Mixed Numbers

✏️ *Solve and write the answer in lowest terms.*

1) $1\frac{1}{8} \times 1\frac{3}{4} =$

2) $3\frac{1}{5} \times 2\frac{2}{7} =$

3) $2\frac{1}{8} \times 1\frac{2}{9} =$

4) $2\frac{3}{8} \times 2\frac{2}{5} =$

5) $1\frac{1}{2} \times 5\frac{2}{3} =$

6) $3\frac{1}{2} \times 6\frac{2}{3} =$

7) $9\frac{1}{2} \times 2\frac{1}{6} =$

8) $2\frac{5}{8} \times 8\frac{3}{5} =$

9) $3\frac{4}{5} \times 4\frac{2}{3} =$

10) $5\frac{1}{3} \times 2\frac{2}{7} =$

11) $6\frac{1}{3} \times 3\frac{3}{4} =$

12) $7\frac{2}{3} \times 1\frac{8}{9} =$

13) $8\frac{1}{2} \times 2\frac{1}{6} =$

14) $4\frac{1}{5} \times 8\frac{2}{3} =$

15) $3\frac{1}{8} \times 5\frac{2}{3} =$

16) $2\frac{2}{7} \times 6\frac{2}{5} =$

17) $2\frac{3}{8} \times 7\frac{2}{3} =$

18) $1\frac{7}{8} \times 8\frac{2}{3} =$

19) $9\frac{1}{2} \times 3\frac{1}{5} =$

20) $2\frac{5}{8} \times 4\frac{1}{3} =$

21) $6\frac{1}{3} \times 3\frac{2}{5} =$

22) $5\frac{3}{4} \times 2\frac{2}{7} =$

23) $9\frac{1}{4} \times 2\frac{1}{3} =$

24) $3\frac{3}{7} \times 7\frac{2}{5} =$

25) $4\frac{1}{4} \times 3\frac{2}{5} =$

26) $7\frac{2}{3} \times 3\frac{2}{5} =$

bit.ly/3aPy7XJ

Find more at

Multiplying Mixed Numbers - Answers

✎ *Solve and write the answer in lowest terms.*

1) $1\frac{1}{8} \times 1\frac{3}{4} = 1\frac{31}{32}$

2) $3\frac{1}{5} \times 2\frac{2}{7} = 7\frac{11}{35}$

3) $2\frac{1}{8} \times 1\frac{2}{9} = 2\frac{43}{72}$

4) $2\frac{3}{8} \times 2\frac{2}{5} = 5\frac{7}{10}$

5) $1\frac{1}{2} \times 5\frac{2}{3} = 8\frac{1}{2}$

6) $3\frac{1}{2} \times 6\frac{2}{3} = 23\frac{1}{3}$

7) $9\frac{1}{2} \times 2\frac{1}{6} = 20\frac{7}{12}$

8) $2\frac{5}{8} \times 8\frac{3}{5} = 22\frac{23}{40}$

9) $3\frac{4}{5} \times 4\frac{2}{3} = 17\frac{11}{15}$

10) $5\frac{1}{3} \times 2\frac{2}{7} = 12\frac{4}{21}$

11) $6\frac{1}{3} \times 3\frac{3}{4} = 23\frac{3}{4}$

12) $7\frac{2}{3} \times 1\frac{8}{9} = 14\frac{13}{27}$

13) $8\frac{1}{2} \times 2\frac{1}{6} = 18\frac{5}{12}$

14) $4\frac{1}{5} \times 8\frac{2}{3} = 36\frac{2}{5}$

15) $3\frac{1}{8} \times 5\frac{2}{3} = 17\frac{17}{24}$

16) $2\frac{2}{7} \times 6\frac{2}{5} = 14\frac{22}{35}$

17) $2\frac{3}{8} \times 7\frac{2}{3} = 18\frac{5}{24}$

18) $1\frac{7}{8} \times 8\frac{2}{3} = 16\frac{1}{4}$

19) $9\frac{1}{2} \times 3\frac{1}{5} = 30\frac{2}{5}$

20) $2\frac{5}{8} \times 4\frac{1}{3} = 11\frac{3}{8}$

21) $6\frac{1}{3} \times 3\frac{2}{5} = 21\frac{8}{15}$

22) $5\frac{3}{4} \times 2\frac{2}{7} = 13\frac{1}{7}$

23) $9\frac{1}{4} \times 2\frac{1}{3} = 21\frac{7}{12}$

24) $3\frac{3}{7} \times 7\frac{2}{5} = 25\frac{13}{35}$

25) $4\frac{1}{4} \times 3\frac{2}{5} = 14\frac{9}{20}$

26) $7\frac{2}{3} \times 3\frac{2}{5} = 26\frac{1}{15}$

Dividing Mixed Numbers

✏️ *Solve and write the answer in lowest terms.*

1) $9\frac{1}{2} \div 2\frac{3}{5} =$

2) $2\frac{3}{8} \div 1\frac{2}{5} =$

3) $5\frac{3}{4} \div 2\frac{2}{7} =$

4) $8\frac{1}{3} \div 4\frac{1}{4} =$

5) $7\frac{2}{5} \div 3\frac{3}{4} =$

6) $2\frac{4}{5} \div 3\frac{2}{3} =$

7) $8\frac{3}{5} \div 4\frac{3}{4} =$

8) $6\frac{3}{4} \div 2\frac{2}{9} =$

9) $5\frac{2}{7} \div 2\frac{2}{9} =$

10) $2\frac{2}{5} \div 3\frac{3}{5} =$

11) $4\frac{3}{7} \div 1\frac{7}{8} =$

12) $2\frac{5}{7} \div 2\frac{4}{5} =$

13) $8\frac{3}{5} \div 6\frac{1}{5} =$

14) $2\frac{5}{8} \div 1\frac{8}{9} =$

15) $5\frac{6}{7} \div 2\frac{3}{4} =$

16) $1\frac{3}{5} \div 2\frac{3}{8} =$

17) $5\frac{3}{4} \div 3\frac{2}{5} =$

18) $2\frac{3}{4} \div 3\frac{1}{5} =$

19) $3\frac{2}{3} \div 1\frac{2}{5} =$

20) $4\frac{1}{4} \div 2\frac{2}{3} =$

21) $3\frac{5}{6} \div 2\frac{4}{5} =$

22) $2\frac{1}{8} \div 1\frac{3}{4} =$

23) $5\frac{1}{2} \div 2\frac{2}{5} =$

24) $3\frac{4}{7} \div 2\frac{2}{3} =$

25) $2\frac{4}{5} \div 3\frac{5}{6} =$

26) $2\frac{3}{7} \div 3\frac{2}{3} =$

Find more at
bit.ly/2KLPk9k

Dividing Mixed Numbers - Answers

✍ *Solve and write the answer in lowest terms.*

1) $9\frac{1}{2} \div 2\frac{3}{5} = 3\frac{17}{26}$

2) $2\frac{3}{8} \div 1\frac{2}{5} = 1\frac{39}{56}$

3) $5\frac{3}{4} \div 2\frac{2}{7} = 2\frac{33}{64}$

4) $8\frac{1}{3} \div 4\frac{1}{4} = 1\frac{49}{51}$

5) $7\frac{2}{5} \div 3\frac{3}{4} = 1\frac{73}{75}$

6) $2\frac{4}{5} \div 3\frac{2}{3} = \frac{42}{55}$

7) $8\frac{3}{5} \div 4\frac{3}{4} = 1\frac{77}{95}$

8) $6\frac{3}{4} \div 2\frac{2}{9} = 3\frac{3}{80}$

9) $5\frac{2}{7} \div 2\frac{2}{9} = 2\frac{53}{140}$

10) $2\frac{2}{5} \div 3\frac{3}{5} = \frac{2}{3}$

11) $4\frac{3}{7} \div 1\frac{7}{8} = 2\frac{88}{105}$

12) $2\frac{5}{7} \div 2\frac{4}{5} = \frac{95}{98}$

13) $8\frac{3}{5} \div 6\frac{1}{5} = 1\frac{12}{31}$

14) $2\frac{5}{8} \div 1\frac{8}{9} = 1\frac{53}{136}$

15) $5\frac{6}{7} \div 2\frac{3}{4} = 2\frac{10}{77}$

16) $1\frac{3}{5} \div 2\frac{3}{8} = \frac{64}{95}$

17) $5\frac{3}{4} \div 3\frac{2}{5} = 1\frac{47}{68}$

18) $2\frac{3}{4} \div 3\frac{1}{5} = \frac{55}{64}$

19) $3\frac{2}{3} \div 1\frac{2}{5} = 2\frac{13}{21}$

20) $4\frac{1}{4} \div 2\frac{2}{3} = 1\frac{19}{32}$

21) $3\frac{5}{6} \div 2\frac{4}{5} = 1\frac{31}{84}$

22) $2\frac{1}{8} \div 1\frac{3}{4} = 1\frac{3}{14}$

23) $5\frac{1}{2} \div 2\frac{2}{5} = 2\frac{7}{24}$

24) $3\frac{4}{7} \div 2\frac{2}{3} = 1\frac{19}{56}$

25) $2\frac{4}{5} \div 3\frac{5}{6} = \frac{84}{115}$

26) $2\frac{3}{7} \div 3\frac{2}{3} = \frac{51}{77}$

bit.ly/2KLPk9k
Find more at

Comparing Decimals

✎ *Compare. Use* $>$*,* $=$*, and* $<$

1) 0.88 ☐ 0.088

2) 0.56 ☐ 0.57

3) 0.99 ☐ 0.89

4) 1.55 ☐ 1.65

5) 1.58 ☐ 1.75

6) 2.91 ☐ 2.85

7) 14.56 ☐ 1.456

8) 17.85 ☐ 17.89

9) 21.52 ☐ 21.052

10) 11.12 ☐ 11.03

11) 9.650 ☐ 9.65

12) 8.578 ☐ 8.568

13) 3.15 ☐ 0.315

14) 16.61 ☐ 16.16

15) 18.581 ☐ 8.991

16) 25.05 ☐ 2.505

17) 4.55 ☐ 4.65

18) 0.158 ☐ 1.58

19) 0.881 ☐ 0.871

20) 0.505 ☐ 0.510

21) 0.772 ☐ 0.777

22) 0.5 ☐ 0.500

23) 16.89 ☐ 15.89

24) 12.25 ☐ 12.35

25) 5.82 ☐ 5.69

26) 1.320 ☐ 1.032

27) 0.082 ☐ 0.088

28) 0.99 ☐ 0.099

29) 2.560 ☐ 1.950

30) 0.770 ☐ 0.707

31) 15.54 ☐ 1.554

32) 0.323 ☐ 0.332

bit.ly/2WHt2Za

Find more at

Comparing Decimals – Answers

✎ **Compare. Use >, =, and <**

1) $0.88 > 0.088$

2) $0.56 < 0.57$

3) $0.99 > 0.89$

4) $1.55 < 1.65$

5) $1.58 < 1.75$

6) $2.91 > 2.85$

7) $14.56 > 1.456$

8) $17.85 < 17.89$

9) $21.52 > 21.052$

10) $11.12 > 11.03$

11) $9.650 = 9.65$

12) $8.578 > 8.568$

13) $3.15 > 0.315$

14) $16.61 > 16.16$

15) $18.581 > 8.991$

16) $25.05 > 2.505$

17) $4.55 < 4.65$

18) $0.158 < 1.58$

19) $0.881 > 0.871$

20) $0.505 < 0.510$

21) $0.772 < 0.777$

22) $0.5 = 0.500$

23) $16.89 > 15.89$

24) $12.25 < 12.35$

25) $5.82 > 5.69$

26) $1.320 > 1.032$

27) $0.082 < 0.088$

28) $0.99 > 0.099$

29) $2.560 > 1.950$

30) $0.770 > 0.707$

31) $15.54 > 1.554$

32) $0.323 < 0.332$

Rounding Decimals

✎ *Round each number to the underlined place value.*

1) 2.814 =

2) 3.562 =

3) 12.125 =

4) 15.5 =

5) 1.981 =

6) 14.215 =

7) 17.548 =

8) 25.508 =

9) 31.089 =

10) 69.345 =

11) 9.457 =

12) 12.901 =

13) 2.658 =

14) 32.565 =

15) 6.058 =

16) 98.108 =

17) 27.705 =

18) 36.75 =

19) 9.08 =

20) 7.185 =

21) 22.547 =

22) 66.098 =

23) 87.75 =

24) 18.541 =

25) 10.258 =

26) 13.456 =

27) 71.084 =

28) 29.23 =

29) 45.55 =

30) 91.08 =

31) 83.433 =

32) 74.64 =

bit.ly/3mKEluf

Find more at

Rounding Decimals - Answers

✍ *Round each number to the underlined place value.*

1) $\underline{2}.814 = 3$

2) $3.5\underline{6}2 = 3.56$

3) $12.1\underline{2}5 = 12.13$

4) $1\underline{5}.5 = 16$

5) $1.9\underline{8}1 = 1.98$

6) $14.\underline{2}15 = 14.2$

7) $17.5\underline{4}8 = 17.55$

8) $25.5\underline{0}8 = 25.51$

9) $3\underline{1}.089 = 31$

10) $69.\underline{3}45 = 69.3$

11) $9.4\underline{5}7 = 9.46$

12) $1\underline{2}.901 = 13$

13) $2.6\underline{5}8 = 2.66$

14) $32.\underline{5}65 = 32.6$

15) $6.0\underline{5}8 = 6.06$

16) $98.1\underline{0}8 = 98.11$

17) $27.\underline{7}05 = 27.7$

18) $3\underline{6}.75 = 37$

19) $9.\underline{0}8 = 9.1$

20) $7.\underline{1}85 = 7.2$

21) $22.5\underline{4}7 = 22.55$

22) $66.\underline{0}98 = 66.1$

23) $8\underline{7}.75 = 88$

24) $18.\underline{5}41 = 18.5$

25) $10.2\underline{5}8 = 10.26$

26) $13.\underline{4}56 = 13.5$

27) $71.0\underline{8}4 = 71.08$

28) $2\underline{9}.23 = 29$

29) $45.\underline{5}5 = 45.6$

30) $9\underline{1}.08 = 91$

31) $8\underline{3}.433 = 83$

32) $74.\underline{6}4 = 74.6$

Adding and Subtracting Decimals

✍ *Solve.*

1) $15.63 + 19.64 =$

2) $16.38 + 17.59 =$

3) $75.31 - 59.69 =$

4) $49.38 - 29.89 =$

5) $24.32 + 26.45 =$

6) $36.25 + 18.37 =$

7) $47.85 - 35.12 =$

8) $85.65 - 67.48 =$

9) $25.49 + 34.18 =$

10) $19.99 + 48.66 =$

11) $46.32 - 27.77 =$

12) $54.62 - 48.12 =$

13) $24.42 + 16.54 =$

14) $52.13 + 12.32 =$

15) $82.36 - 78.65 =$

16) $64.12 - 49.15 =$

17) $36.41 + 24.52 =$

18) $85.96 - 74.63 =$

19) $52.62 - 42.54 =$

20) $21.20 + 24.58 =$

21) $32.15 + 17.17 =$

22) $96.32 - 85.54 =$

23) $89.78 - 69.85 =$

24) $29.28 + 39.79 =$

25) $11.11 + 19.99 =$

26) $28.82 + 20.88 =$

27) $63.14 - 28.91 =$

28) $56.61 - 49.72 =$

29) $26.13 + 31.13 =$

30) $30.19 + 20.87 =$

31) $66.24 - 59.10 =$

32) $89.31 - 72.17 =$

bit.ly/38uyUdx

Find more at

Adding and Subtracting Decimals - Answers

✎ *Solve.*

1) $15.63 + 19.64 = 35.27$

2) $16.38 + 17.59 = 33.97$

3) $75.31 - 59.69 = 15.62$

4) $49.38 - 29.89 = 19.49$

5) $24.32 + 26.45 = 50.77$

6) $36.25 + 18.37 = 54.62$

7) $47.85 - 35.12 = 12.73$

8) $85.65 - 67.48 = 18.17$

9) $25.49 + 34.18 = 59.67$

10) $19.99 + 48.66 = 68.65$

11) $46.32 - 27.77 = 18.55$

12) $54.62 - 48.12 = 6.5$

13) $24.42 + 16.54 = 40.96$

14) $52.13 + 12.32 = 64.45$

15) $82.36 - 78.65 = 3.71$

16) $64.12 - 49.15 = 14.97$

17) $36.41 + 24.52 = 60.93$

18) $85.96 - 74.63 = 11.33$

19) $52.62 - 42.54 = 10.08$

20) $21.20 + 24.58 = 45.78$

21) $32.15 + 17.17 = 49.32$

22) $96.32 - 85.54 = 10.78$

23) $89.78 - 69.85 = 19.93$

24) $29.28 + 39.79 = 69.07$

25) $11.11 + 19.99 = 31.1$

26) $28.82 + 20.88 = 49.7$

27) $63.14 - 28.91 = 34.23$

28) $56.61 - 49.72 = 6.89$

29) $26.13 + 31.13 = 57.26$

30) $30.19 + 20.87 = 51.06$

31) $66.24 - 59.10 = 7.14$

32) $89.31 - 72.17 = 17.14$

Find more at   bit.ly/38uyUdx

Multiplying and Dividing Decimals

✏️ *Solve.*

1) $11.2 \times 0.4 =$

2) $13.5 \times 0.8 =$

3) $42.2 \div 2 =$

4) $54.6 \div 6 =$

5) $23.1 \times 0.3 =$

6) $1.2 \times 0.7 =$

7) $5.5 \div 0.5 =$

8) $64.8 \div 8 =$

9) $1.4 \times 0.5 =$

10) $4.5 \times 0.3 =$

11) $88.8 \div 4 =$

12) $10.5 \div 5 =$

13) $2.2 \times 0.3 =$

14) $0.2 \times 0.52 =$

15) $95.7 \div 100 =$

16) $36.6 \div 6 =$

17) $3.2 \times 2 =$

18) $4.1 \times 0.5 =$

19) $68.4 \div 2 =$

20) $27.9 \div 9 =$

21) $3.5 \times 4 =$

22) $4.8 \times 0.5 =$

23) $6.4 \div 4 =$

24) $72.8 \div 0.8 =$

25) $1.8 \times 3 =$

26) $6.5 \times 0.2 =$

27) $93.6 \div 3 =$

28) $45.15 \div 0.5 =$

29) $13.2 \times 0.4 =$

30) $11.2 \times 5 =$

31) $7.2 \div 0.8 =$

32) $96.4 \div 0.2 =$

bit.ly/34DZ0cS

Find more at

Multiplying and Dividing Decimals - Answers

✍ *Solve.*

1) $11.2 \times 0.4 = 4.48$

2) $13.5 \times 0.8 = 10.8$

3) $42.2 \div 2 = 21.1$

4) $54.6 \div 6 = 9.1$

5) $23.1 \times 0.3 = 6.93$

6) $1.2 \times 0.7 = 0.84$

7) $5.5 \div 5 = 1.1$

8) $64.8 \div 8 = 8.1$

9) $1.4 \times 0.5 = 0.7$

10) $4.5 \times 0.3 = 1.35$

11) $88.8 \div 4 = 22.2$

12) $10.5 \div 5 = 2.1$

13) $2.2 \times 0.3 = 0.66$

14) $0.2 \times 0.52 = 0.104$

15) $95.7 \div 100 = 0.957$

16) $36.6 \div 6 = 6.1$

17) $3.2 \times 2 = 6.4$

18) $4.1 \times 0.5 = 2.05$

19) $68.4 \div 2 = 34.2$

20) $27.9 \div 9 = 3.1$

21) $3.5 \times 4 = 14$

22) $4.8 \times 0.5 = 2.4$

23) $6.4 \div 4 = 1.6$

24) $72.8 \div 0.8 = 91$

25) $1.8 \times 3 = 5.4$

26) $6.5 \times 0.2 = 1.3$

27) $93.6 \div 3 = 31.2$

28) $45.15 \div 0.5 = 90.3$

29) $13.2 \times 0.4 = 5.28$

30) $11.2 \times 5 = 56$

31) $7.2 \div 0.8 = 9$

32) $96.4 \div 0.2 = 482$

bit.ly/34DZ0cS

Find more at

Adding and Subtracting Integers

✎ *Solve.*

1) $-(8) + 13 =$

2) $17 - (-12 - 8) =$

3) $(-15) + (-4) =$

4) $(-14) + (-8) + 9 =$

5) $-(23) + 19 =$

6) $(-7 + 5) - 9 =$

7) $28 + (-32) =$

8) $(-11) + (-9) + 5 =$

9) $25 - (8 - 7) =$

10) $-(29) + 17 =$

11) $(-38) + (-3) + 29 =$

12) $15 - (-7 + 9) =$

13) $24 - (8 - 2) =$

14) $(-7 + 4) - 9 =$

15) $(-17) + (-3) + 9 =$

16) $(-26) + (-7) + 8 =$

17) $(-9) + (-11) =$

18) $8 - (-23 - 13) =$

19) $(-16) + (-2) =$

20) $25 - (7 - 4) =$

21) $23 + (-12) =$

22) $(-18) + (-6) =$

23) $17 - (-21 - 7) =$

24) $-(28) - (-16) + 5 =$

25) $(-9 + 4) - 8 =$

26) $(-28) + (-6) + 17 =$

27) $-(21) - (-15) + 9 =$

28) $(-31) + (-6) =$

29) $(-17) + (-11) + 14 =$

30) $(-29) + (-10) + 13 =$

31) $-(24) - (-12) + 5 =$

32) $8 - (-19 - 10) =$

bit.ly/3aKx5vI

Find more at

Adding and Subtracting Integers - Answers

✎ *Solve.*

1) $-(8) + 13 = 5$

2) $17 - (-12 - 8) = 37$

3) $(-15) + (-4) = -19$

4) $(-14) + (-8) + 9 = -13$

5) $-(23) + 19 = -4$

6) $(-7 + 5) - 9 = -11$

7) $28 + (-32) = -4$

8) $(-11) + (-9) + 5 = -15$

9) $25 - (8 - 7) = 24$

10) $-(29) + 17 = -12$

11) $(-38) + (-3) + 29 = -12$

12) $15 - (-7 + 9) = 13$

13) $24 - (8 - 2) = 18$

14) $(-7 + 4) - 9 = -12$

15) $(-17) + (-3) + 9 = -11$

16) $(-26) + (-7) + 8 = -25$

17) $(-9) + (-11) = -20$

18) $8 - (-23 - 13) = 44$

19) $(-16) + (-2) = -18$

20) $25 - (7 - 4) = 22$

21) $23 + (-12) = 11$

22) $(-18) + (-6) = -24$

23) $17 - (-21 - 7) = 45$

24) $-(28) - (-16) + 5 = -7$

25) $(-9 + 4) - 8 = -13$

26) $(-28) + (-6) + 17 = -17$

27) $-(21) - (-15) + 9 = 3$

28) $(-31) + (-6) = -37$

29) $(-17) + (-11) + 14 = -14$

30) $(-29) + (-10) + 13 = -26$

31) $-(24) - (-12) + 5 = -7$

32) $8 - (-19 - 10) = 37$

Multiplying and Dividing Integers

✎ *Solve.*

1) $(-9) \times (-8) =$

2) $6 \times (-6) =$

3) $49 \div (-7) =$

4) $(-64) \div 8 =$

5) $(4) \times (-6) =$

6) $(-9) \times (-11) =$

7) $(10) \div (-5) =$

8) $144 \div (-12) =$

9) $(10) \times (-2) =$

10) $(-8) \times (-2) \times 5 =$

11) $(8) \div (-2) =$

12) $45 \div (-15) =$

13) $(5) \times (-7) =$

14) $(-6) \times (-5) \times 4 =$

15) $(12) \div (-6) =$

16) $(14) \div (-7) =$

17) $196 \div (-14) =$

18) $(27 - 13) \times (-2) =$

19) $125 \div (-5) =$

20) $66 \div (-6) =$

21) $(-6) \times (-5) \times 3 =$

22) $(15 - 6) \times (-3) =$

23) $(32 - 24) \div (-4) =$

24) $72 \div (-6) =$

25) $(-14 + 8) \times (-7) =$

26) $(-3) \times (-9) \times 3 =$

27) $84 \div (-12) =$

28) $(-12) \times (-10) =$

29) $25 \times (-4) =$

30) $(-3) \times (-5) \times 5 =$

31) $(15) \div (-3) =$

32) $(-18) \div (3) =$

bit.ly/3pjQW98
Find more at

Multiplying and Dividing Integers - Answers

✍ *Solve.*

1) $(-9) \times (-8) = 72$

2) $6 \times (-6) = -36$

3) $49 \div (-7) = -7$

4) $(-64) \div 8 = -8$

5) $(4) \times (-6) = -24$

6) $(-9) \times (-11) = 99$

7) $(10) \div (-5) = -2$

8) $144 \div (-12) = -12$

9) $(10) \times (-2) = -20$

10) $(-8) \times (-2) \times 5 = 80$

11) $(8) \div (-2) = -4$

12) $45 \div (-15) = -3$

13) $(5) \times (-7) = -35$

14) $(-6) \times (-5) \times 5 = 150$

15) $(12) \div (-6) = -2$

16) $(14) \div (-7) = -2$

17) $196 \div (-14) = -14$

18) $(27 - 13) \times (-2) = -28$

19) $125 \div (-5) = -25$

20) $66 \div (-6) = -11$

21) $(-6) \times (-5) \times 3 = 90$

22) $(15 - 6) \times (-3) = -27$

23) $(32 - 24) \div (-4) = -2$

24) $72 \div (-6) = -12$

25) $(-14 + 8) \times (-7) = 42$

26) $(-3) \times (-9) \times 3 = 81$

27) $84 \div (-12) = -7$

28) $(-12) \times (-10) = 120$

29) $25 \times (-4) = -100$

30) $(-3) \times (-5) \times 5 = 75$

31) $(15) \div (-3) = -5$

32) $(-18) \div (3) = -6$

Order of Operation

✍ *Calculate.*

1) $18 + (32 \div 4) =$

2) $(3 \times 8) \div (-2) =$

3) $67 - (4 \times 8) =$

4) $(-11) \times (8 - 3) =$

5) $(18 - 7) \times (6) =$

6) $(6 \times 10) \div (12 + 3) =$

7) $(13 \times 2) - (24 \div 6) =$

8) $(-5) + (4 \times 3) + 8 =$

9) $(4 \times 2^3) + (16 - 9) =$

10) $(3^2 \times 7) \div (-2 + 1) =$

11) $[-2(48 \div 2^3)] - 6 =$

12) $(-4) + (7 \times 8) + 18 =$

13) $(3 \times 7) + (16 - 7) =$

14) $[3^3 \times (48 \div 2^3)] \div (-2) =$

15) $(14 \times 3) - (3^4 \div 9) =$

16) $(96 \div 12) \times (-3) =$

17) $(48 \div 2^2) \times (-2) =$

18) $(56 \div 7) \times (-5) =$

19) $(-2^2) + (7 \times 9) - 21 =$

20) $(2^4 - 9) \times (-6) =$

21) $[4^3 \times (50 \div 5^2)] \div (-16) =$

22) $(3^2 \times 4^2) \div (-4 + 2) =$

23) $6^2 - (-6 \times 4) + 3 =$

24) $4^2 - (5^2 \times 3) =$

25) $(-4) + (12^2 \div 3^2) - 7^2 =$

26) $(3^2 \times 5) + (-5^2 - 9) =$

27) $2[(3^2 \times 5) \times (-6)] =$

28) $(11^2 - 2^2) - (-7^2) =$

29) $(2^3 \times 3) - (49 \div 7) =$

30) $3[(3^2 \times 5) + (25 \div 5)] =$

31) $(6^2 \times 5) \div (-5) =$

32) $2^2[(6^3 \div 12) - (3^4 \div 27)] =$

bit.ly/37LBw7X

Find more at

Order of Operation - Answers

✎ *Calculate.*

1) $18 + (32 \div 4) = 26$

2) $(3 \times 8) \div (-2) = -12$

3) $67 - (4 \times 8) = 35$

4) $(-11) \times (8 - 3) = -55$

5) $(18 - 7) \times (6) = 66$

6) $(6 \times 10) \div (12 + 3) = 4$

7) $(13 \times 2) - (24 \div 6) = 22$

8) $(-5) + (4 \times 3) + 8 = 15$

9) $(4 \times 2^3) + (16 - 9) = 39$

10) $(3^2 \times 7) \div (-2 + 1) = -63$

11) $[-2(48 \div 2^3)] - 6 = -18$

12) $(-4) + (7 \times 8) + 18 = 70$

13) $(3 \times 7) + (16 - 7) = 30$

14) $[3^3 \times (48 \div 2^3)] \div (-2) = -81$

15) $(14 \times 3) - (3^4 \div 9) = 33$

16) $(96 \div 12) \times (-3) = -24$

17) $(48 \div 2^2) \times (-2) = -24$

18) $(56 \div 7) \times (-5) = -40$

19) $(-2^2) + (7 \times 9) - 21 = 38$

20) $(2^4 - 9) \times (-6) = -42$

21) $[4^3 \times (50 \div 5^2)] \div (-16) = -8$

22) $(3^2 \times 4^2) \div (-4 + 2) = -72$

23) $6^2 - (-6 \times 4) + 3 = 63$

24) $4^2 - (5^2 \times 3) = -59$

25) $(-4) + (12^2 \div 3^2) - 7^2 = -37$

26) $(3^2 \times 5) + (-5^2 - 9) = 11$

27) $2[(3^2 \times 5) \times (-6)] = -540$

28) $(11^2 - 2^2) - (-7^2) = 166$

29) $(2^3 \times 3) - (49 \div 7) = 17$

30) $3[(3^2 \times 5) + (25 \div 5)] = 150$

31) $(6^2 \times 5) \div (-5) = -36$

32) $2^2[(6^3 \div 12) - (3^4 \div 27) = 60$

bit.ly/37LBw7X

Find more at

Integers and Absolute Value

✎ *Calculate.*

1) $5 - |8 - 12| =$

2) $|15| - \dfrac{|-16|}{4} =$

3) $\dfrac{|9 \times -6|}{18} \times \dfrac{|-24|}{8} =$

4) $|13 \times 3| + \dfrac{|-72|}{9} =$

5) $4 - |11 - 18| - |3| =$

6) $|18| - \dfrac{|-12|}{4} =$

7) $\dfrac{|5 \times -8|}{10} \times \dfrac{|-22|}{11} =$

8) $|9 \times 3| + \dfrac{|-36|}{4} =$

9) $|-42 + 7| \times \dfrac{|-2 \times 5|}{10} =$

10) $6 - |17 - 11| - |5| =$

11) $|13| - \dfrac{|-54|}{6} =$

12) $\dfrac{|9 \times -4|}{12} \times \dfrac{|-45|}{9} =$

13) $|-75 + 50| \times \dfrac{|-4 \times 5|}{5} =$

14) $\dfrac{|-26|}{13} \times \dfrac{|-32|}{8} =$

15) $14 - |8 - 18| - |-12| =$

16) $|29| - \dfrac{|-20|}{5} =$

17) $\dfrac{|3 \times 8|}{2} \times \dfrac{|-33|}{3} =$

18) $|-45 + 15| \times \dfrac{|-12 \times 5|}{6} =$

19) $\dfrac{|-50|}{5} \times \dfrac{|-77|}{11} =$

20) $12 - |2 - 7| - |15| =$

21) $|18| - \dfrac{|-45|}{15} =$

22) $\dfrac{|7 \times 8|}{4} \times \dfrac{|-48|}{12} =$

23) $\dfrac{|30 \times 2|}{3} \times |-12| =$

24) $\dfrac{|-36|}{9} \times \dfrac{|-80|}{8} =$

25) $|-35 + 8| \times \dfrac{|-9 \times 5|}{15} =$

26) $|19| - \dfrac{|-18|}{2} =$

27) $14 - |11 - 23| + |2| =$

28) $|-39 + 7| \times \dfrac{|-4 \times 6|}{3} =$

EffortlessMath.com

bit.ly/3aD521u

Find more at

Integers and Absolute Value - Answers

✎ *Calculate.*

1) $5 - |8 - 12| = 1$

2) $|15| - \frac{|-16|}{4} = 11$

3) $\frac{|9 \times -6|}{18} \times \frac{|-24|}{8} = 9$

4) $|13 \times 3| + \frac{|-72|}{9} = 47$

5) $4 - |11 - 18| - |3| = -6$

6) $|18| - \frac{|-12|}{4} = 15$

7) $\frac{|5 \times -8|}{10} \times \frac{|-22|}{11} = 8$

8) $|9 \times 3| + \frac{|-36|}{4} = 36$

9) $|-42 + 7| \times \frac{|-2 \times 5|}{10} = 35$

10) $6 - |17 - 11| - |5| = -5$

11) $|13| - \frac{|-54|}{6} = 4$

12) $\frac{|9 \times -4|}{12} \times \frac{|-45|}{9} = 15$

13) $|-75 + 50| \times \frac{|-4 \times 5|}{5} = 100$

14) $\frac{|-26|}{13} \times \frac{|-32|}{8} = 8$

15) $14 - |8 - 18| - |-12| = -8$

16) $|29| - \frac{|-20|}{5} = 25$

17) $\frac{|3 \times 8|}{2} \times \frac{|-33|}{3} = 132$

18) $|-45 + 15| \times \frac{|-12 \times 5|}{6} = 300$

19) $\frac{|-50|}{5} \times \frac{|-77|}{11} = 70$

20) $12 - |2 - 7| - |15| = -8$

21) $|18| - \frac{|-45|}{15} = 15$

22) $\frac{|7 \times 8|}{4} \times \frac{|-48|}{12} = 56$

23) $\frac{|30 \times 2|}{3} \times |-12| = 240$

24) $\frac{|-36|}{9} \times \frac{|-80|}{8} = 40$

25) $|-35 + 8| \times \frac{|-9 \times 5|}{15} = 81$

26) $|19| - \frac{|-18|}{2} = 10$

27) $14 - |11 - 23| + |2| = 4$

28) $|-39 + 7| \times \frac{|-4 \times 6|}{3} = 256$

bit.ly/3aD521u

Find more at

Simplifying Ratios

✎ *Simplify each ratio.*

1) $3:27 =$ ___ : ___

2) $2:8 =$ ___ : ___

3) $\frac{4}{28} = -$

4) $\frac{16}{40} = -$

5) $10:30 =$ ___ : ___

6) $5:30 =$ ___ : ___

7) $\frac{34}{38} = -$

8) $\frac{45}{63} = -$

9) $10:45 =$ ___ : ___

10) $20:30 =$ ___ : ___

11) $\frac{40}{64} = -$

12) $\frac{10}{110} = -$

13) $8:12 =$ ___ : ___

14) $16:20 =$ ___ : ___

15) $\frac{24}{48} = -$

16) $\frac{21}{77} = -$

17) $8:24 =$ ___ : ___

18) 9 to $36 =$ ___ : ___

19) $\frac{64}{72} = -$

20) $\frac{45}{60} = -$

21) $12:15 =$ ___ : ___

22) $18:54 =$ ___ : ___

23) $\frac{36}{54} = -$

24) $\frac{48}{104} = -$

25) $15:75 =$ ___ : ___

26) $16:48 =$ ___ : ___

27) $\frac{15}{65} = -$

28) $\frac{44}{52} = -$

bit.ly/3nKwq0Z

Find more at

Simplifying Ratios - Answers

✎ *Simplify each ratio.*

1) $3:27 = 1:9$

2) $2:8 = 1:4$

3) $\frac{4}{28} = \frac{1}{7}$

4) $\frac{16}{40} = \frac{2}{5}$

5) $10:30 = 1:3$

6) $5:30 = 1:6$

7) $\frac{34}{38} = \frac{17}{19}$

8) $\frac{45}{63} = \frac{5}{7}$

9) $10:45 = 2:9$

10) $20:30 = 2:3$

11) $\frac{40}{64} = \frac{5}{8}$

12) $\frac{10}{110} = \frac{1}{11}$

13) $8:12 = 2:3$

14) $16:20 = 4:5$

15) $\frac{24}{48} = \frac{1}{2}$

16) $\frac{21}{77} = \frac{3}{11}$

17) $8:24 = 1:6$

18) $9 \text{ to } 36 = 1 \text{ to } 4$

19) $\frac{64}{72} = \frac{8}{9}$

20) $\frac{45}{60} = \frac{3}{4}$

21) $12:15 = 4:5$

22) $18:54 = 1:3$

23) $\frac{36}{54} = \frac{2}{3}$

24) $\frac{48}{104} = \frac{6}{13}$

25) $15:75 = 1:5$

26) $16:48 = 1:3$

27) $\frac{15}{65} = \frac{3}{13}$

28) $\frac{44}{52} = \frac{11}{13}$

bit.ly/3nKwq0Z
Find more at
EffortlessMath.com

Proportional Ratios

✍ *Solve each proportion for x.*

1) $\frac{4}{7} = \frac{16}{x}$, $x =$ _____

2) $\frac{4}{9} = \frac{x}{18}$, $x =$ _____

3) $\frac{3}{5} = \frac{24}{x}$, $x =$ _____

4) $\frac{3}{10} = \frac{x}{50}$, $x =$ _____

5) $\frac{3}{11} = \frac{15}{x}$, $x =$ _____

6) $\frac{6}{15} = \frac{x}{45}$, $x =$ _____

7) $\frac{6}{19} = \frac{12}{x}$, $x =$ _____

8) $\frac{7}{16} = \frac{x}{32}$, $x =$ _____

9) $\frac{18}{21} = \frac{54}{x}$, $x =$ _____

10) $\frac{13}{15} = \frac{39}{x}$, $x =$ _____

11) $\frac{9}{13} = \frac{72}{x}$, $x =$ _____

12) $\frac{8}{30} = \frac{x}{180}$, $x =$ _____

13) $\frac{3}{19} = \frac{9}{x}$, $x =$ _____

14) $\frac{1}{3} = \frac{x}{90}$, $x =$ _____

15) $\frac{25}{45} = \frac{x}{9}$, $x =$ _____

16) $\frac{1}{6} = \frac{9}{x}$, $x =$ _____

17) $\frac{7}{9} = \frac{63}{x}$, $x =$ _____

18) $\frac{54}{72} = \frac{x}{8}$, $x =$ _____

19) $\frac{32}{40} = \frac{4}{x}$, $x =$ _____

20) $\frac{21}{42} = \frac{x}{6}$, $x =$ _____

21) $\frac{56}{72} = \frac{7}{x}$, $x =$ _____

22) $\frac{1}{14} = \frac{x}{42}$, $x =$ _____

23) $\frac{5}{7} = \frac{75}{x}$, $x =$ _____

24) $\frac{30}{48} = \frac{x}{8}$, $x =$ _____

25) $\frac{36}{88} = \frac{9}{x}$, $x =$ _____

26) $\frac{62}{68} = \frac{x}{34}$, $x =$ _____

27) $\frac{42}{60} = \frac{x}{10}$, $x =$ _____

28) $\frac{8}{9} = \frac{x}{108}$, $x =$ _____

29) $\frac{46}{69} = \frac{x}{3}$, $x =$ _____

30) $\frac{99}{121} = \frac{x}{11}$, $x =$ _____

31) $\frac{19}{21} = \frac{x}{63}$, $x =$ _____

32) $\frac{11}{12} = \frac{x}{48}$, $x =$ _____

bit.ly/37GHQxp

Find more at

Proportional Ratios - Answers

🖱 **Solve each proportion for x.**

1) $\frac{4}{7} = \frac{16}{x}$, $x = 28$

2) $\frac{4}{9} = \frac{x}{18}$, $x = 8$

3) $\frac{3}{5} = \frac{24}{x}$, $x = 40$

4) $\frac{3}{10} = \frac{x}{50}$, $x = 15$

5) $\frac{3}{11} = \frac{15}{x}$, $x = 55$

6) $\frac{6}{15} = \frac{x}{45}$, $x = 18$

7) $\frac{6}{19} = \frac{12}{x}$, $x = 38$

8) $\frac{7}{16} = \frac{x}{32}$, $x = 14$

9) $\frac{18}{21} = \frac{54}{x}$, $x = 63$

10) $\frac{13}{15} = \frac{39}{x}$, $x = 45$

11) $\frac{9}{13} = \frac{72}{x}$, $x = 104$

12) $\frac{8}{30} = \frac{x}{180}$, $x = 48$

13) $\frac{3}{19} = \frac{9}{x}$, $x = 57$

14) $\frac{1}{3} = \frac{x}{90}$, $x = 30$

15) $\frac{25}{45} = \frac{x}{9}$, $x = 5$

16) $\frac{1}{6} = \frac{9}{x}$, $x = 54$

17) $\frac{7}{9} = \frac{63}{x}$, $x = 81$

18) $\frac{54}{72} = \frac{x}{8}$, $x = 6$

19) $\frac{32}{40} = \frac{4}{x}$, $x = 5$

20) $\frac{21}{42} = \frac{x}{6}$, $x = 3$

21) $\frac{56}{72} = \frac{7}{x}$, $x = 9$

22) $\frac{1}{14} = \frac{x}{42}$, $x = 3$

23) $\frac{5}{7} = \frac{75}{x}$, $x = 105$

24) $\frac{30}{48} = \frac{x}{8}$, $x = 5$

25) $\frac{36}{88} = \frac{9}{x}$, $x = 22$

26) $\frac{62}{68} = \frac{x}{34}$, $x = 31$

27) $\frac{42}{60} = \frac{x}{10}$, $x = 7$

28) $\frac{8}{9} = \frac{x}{108}$, $x = 96$

29) $\frac{46}{69} = \frac{x}{3}$, $x = 2$

30) $\frac{99}{121} = \frac{x}{11}$, $x = 9$

31) $\frac{19}{21} = \frac{x}{63}$, $x = 57$

32) $\frac{11}{12} = \frac{x}{48}$, $x = 44$

Create Proportion

✎ *State if each pair of ratios form a proportion.*

1) $\frac{5}{8}$ *and* $\frac{25}{50}$

2) $\frac{2}{11}$ *and* $\frac{4}{22}$

3) $\frac{2}{5}$ *and* $\frac{8}{20}$

4) $\frac{3}{11}$ *and* $\frac{9}{33}$

5) $\frac{5}{10}$ *and* $\frac{15}{30}$

6) $\frac{4}{13}$ *and* $\frac{8}{24}$

7) $\frac{6}{9}$ *and* $\frac{24}{36}$

8) $\frac{7}{12}$ *and* $\frac{14}{20}$

9) $\frac{3}{8}$ *and* $\frac{27}{72}$

10) $\frac{12}{20}$ *and* $\frac{36}{60}$

11) $\frac{11}{12}$ *and* $\frac{55}{60}$

12) $\frac{12}{15}$ *and* $\frac{24}{25}$

13) $\frac{15}{19}$ *and* $\frac{20}{38}$

14) $\frac{10}{14}$ *and* $\frac{40}{56}$

15) $\frac{11}{13}$ *and* $\frac{44}{39}$

16) $\frac{15}{16}$ *and* $\frac{30}{32}$

17) $\frac{17}{19}$ *and* $\frac{34}{48}$

18) $\frac{5}{18}$ *and* $\frac{15}{54}$

19) $\frac{3}{14}$ *and* $\frac{18}{42}$

20) $\frac{7}{11}$ *and* $\frac{14}{32}$

21) $\frac{8}{11}$ *and* $\frac{32}{44}$

22) $\frac{9}{13}$ *and* $\frac{18}{26}$

✎ *Solve.*

23) The ratio of boys to girls in a class is 5:6. If there are 25 boys in the class, how many girls are in that class? _____

24) The ratio of red marbles to blue marbles in a bag is 4:7. If there are 77 marbles in the bag, how many of the marbles are red? _____

25) You can buy 8 cans of green beans at a supermarket for $3.20. How much does it cost to buy 48 cans of green beans? _____

bit.ly/37GHQxp

Find more at

Create Proportion - Answers

 State if each pair of ratios form a proportion.

1) $\frac{5}{8}$ and $\frac{25}{50}$, *No*

2) $\frac{2}{11}$ and $\frac{4}{22}$, *Yes*

3) $\frac{2}{5}$ and $\frac{8}{20}$, *Yes*

4) $\frac{3}{11}$ and $\frac{9}{33}$, *Yes*

5) $\frac{5}{10}$ and $\frac{15}{30}$, *Yes*

6) $\frac{4}{13}$ and $\frac{8}{24}$, *No*

7) $\frac{6}{9}$ and $\frac{24}{36}$, *Yes*

8) $\frac{7}{12}$ and $\frac{14}{20}$, *No*

9) $\frac{3}{8}$ and $\frac{27}{72}$, *Yes*

10) $\frac{12}{20}$ and $\frac{36}{60}$, *Yes*

11) $\frac{11}{12}$ and $\frac{55}{60}$, *Yes*

12) $\frac{12}{15}$ and $\frac{24}{25}$, *No*

13) $\frac{15}{19}$ and $\frac{20}{38}$, *No*

14) $\frac{10}{14}$ and $\frac{40}{56}$, *Yes*

15) $\frac{11}{13}$ and $\frac{44}{39}$, *No*

16) $\frac{15}{16}$ and $\frac{30}{32}$, *Yes*

17) $\frac{17}{19}$ and $\frac{34}{38}$, *Yes*

18) $\frac{5}{18}$ and $\frac{15}{54}$, *Yes*

19) $\frac{3}{14}$ and $\frac{18}{42}$, *No*

20) $\frac{7}{11}$ and $\frac{14}{32}$, *No*

21) $\frac{8}{11}$ and $\frac{32}{44}$, *Yes*

22) $\frac{9}{13}$ and $\frac{18}{26}$, *Yes*

 Solve.

23) The ratio of boys to girls in a class is 5:6. If there are 25 boys in the class, how many girls are in that class? **30 girls**

24) The ratio of red marbles to blue marbles in a bag is 4:7. If there are 77 marbles in the bag, how many of the marbles are red? **28 red marbles**

25) You can buy 8 cans of green beans at a supermarket for $3.20. How much does it cost to buy 48 cans of green beans? **$19.20**

bit.ly/37GHQxp

Find more at

Similarity and Ratios

✎ *Each pair of figures is similar. Find the missing side.*

1)
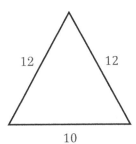 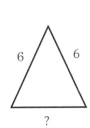

2)
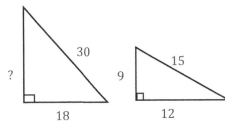

3)
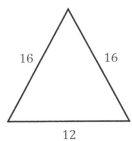 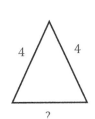

4)
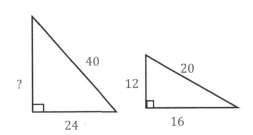

5)
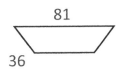

6)
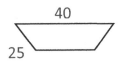

7)
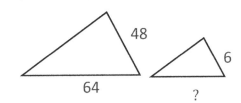

8)
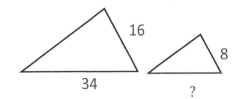

bit.ly/2KKKmcV

Find more at

Similarity and Ratios - Answers

✏️ *Each pair of figures is similar. Find the missing side.*

1) 5

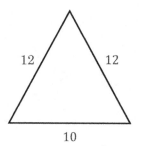

2) 24

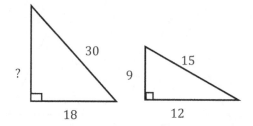

3) 3

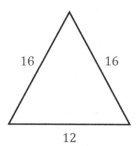

4) 32

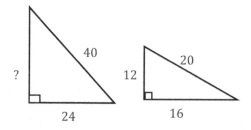

5) 9

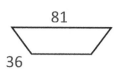

6) 8

7) 8

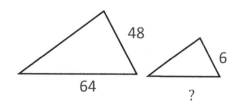

8) 17

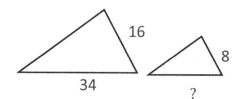

bit.ly/2KKKmcV

Find more at

Simple Interest

✎ *Determine the simple interest for following loans.*

1) $440 at 5% for 6 years. $___

2) $460 at 2.5% for 4 years. $__

3) $500 at 3% for 5 years. $___

4) $550 at 9% for 2 years. $___

5) $690 at 5% for 6 months. $___

6) $620 at 7% for 3 years. $___

7) $650 at 4.5% for 10 years. $___

8) $850 at 4% for 2 years. $___

9) $640 at 7% for 3 years. $___

10) $300 at 9% for 9 months. $___

11) $760 at 8% for 2 years. $__

12) $910 at 5% for 5 years. $___

13) $540 at 3% for 6 years. $___

14) $780 at 2.5% for 4 years. $___

15) $1,600 at 7% for 3 months. $___

16) $310 at 4% for 4 years. $___

17) $950 at 6% for 5 years. $___

18) $280 at 8% for 7 years. $___

19) $310 at 6% for 3 years. $___

20) $990 at 5% for 4 months. $____

21) $380 at 6% for 5 years. $___

22) $580 at 6% for 4 years. $___

23) $1,200 at 4% for5 years. $___

24) $3,100 at 5% for 6 years. $___

25) $5,200 at 8% for 2 years. $___

26) $1,400 at 4% for 3 years. $___

27) $300 at 3% for 8 months. $___

28) $150 at 3.5% for 4 years. $___

29) $170 at 6% for 2 years. $___

30) $940 at 8% for 5 years. $___

31) $960 at 1.5% for 8 years. $__

32) $240 at 5% for 4 months. $___

33) $280 at 2% for 5 years. $___

34) $880 at 3% for 2 years. $___

35) $2,200 at 4.5% for 2 years. $___

36) $2,400 at 7% for 3 years. $___

37) $1,800 at 5% for 6 months. $___

38) $190 at 4% for 2 years. $___

39) $560 at 7% for 4 years. $___

40) $720 at 8% for 2 years. $__

41) $780 at 5% for 8 years. $___

42) $880 at 6% for 3 months. $___

Simple Interest - Answers

✍ *Determine the simple interest for following loans.*

1) $440 at 5% for 6 years. $132
2) $460 at 2.5% for 4 years. $46
3) $500 at 3% for 5 years. $75
4) $550 at 9% for 2 years. $99
5) $690 at 5% for 6 months. $17.25
6) $620 at 7% for 3 years. $130.20
7) $650 at 4.5% for 10 years. $292.50
8) $850 at 4% for 2 years. $68
9) $640 at 7% for 3 years. $134.40
10) $300 at 9% for 9 months. $20.25
11) $760 at 8% for 2 years. $121.60
12) $910 at 5% for 5 years. $227.50
13) $540 at 3% for 6 years. $97.20
14) $780 at 2.5% for 4 years. $78
15) $1,600 at 7% for 3 months. $28
16) $310 at 4% for 4 years. $49.60
17) $950 at 6% for 5 years. $285
18) $280 at 8% for 7 years. $156.80
19) $310 at 6% for 3 years. $55.80
20) $990 at 5% for 4 months. $198
21) $380 at 6% for 5 years. $114

22) $580 at 6% for 4 years. $139.20
23) $1,200 at 4% for 5 years. $240
24) $3,100 at 5% for 6 years. $930
25) $5,200 at 8% for 2 years. $832
26) $1,400 at 4% for 3 years. $168
27) $300 at 3% for 8 months. $6
28) $150 at 3.5% for 4 years. $21
29) $170 at 6% for 2 years. $20.40
30) $940 at 8% for 5 years. $376
31) $960 at 1.5% for 8 years. $115.20
32) $240 at 5% for 4 months. $4
33) $280 at 2% for 5 years. $28
34) $880 at 3% for 2 years. $52.80
35) $2,200 at 4.5% for 2 years. $198
36) $2,400 at 7% for 3 years. $504
37) $1,800 at 5% for 6 months. $45
38) $190 at 4% for 2 years. $15.20
39) $560 at 7% for 4 years. $156.80
40) $720 at 8% for 2 years. $115.20
41) $780 at 5% for 8 years. $312
42) $880 at 6% for 3 months. $13.20

Percent Problems

✍ *Solve each problem.*

1) What is 5 percent of 300? ____

2) What is 15 percent of 600? ____

3) What is 12 percent of 450? ____

4) What is 30 percent of 240? ____

5) What is 60 percent of 850? ____

6) 63 is what percent of 300? ____%

7) 80 is what percent of 400? ____%

8) 70 is what percent of 700? ____%

9) 84 is what percent of 600? ___%

10) 90 is what percent of 300? ___%

11) 24 is what percent of 150? ___%

12) 12 is what percent of 80? ____%

13) 4 is what percent of 50? ____%

14) 110 is what percent of 500? _%

15) 16 is what percent of 400? ___%

16) 39 is what percent of 300? ___%

17) 56 is what percent of 200? ___%

18) 30 is what percent of 500? ___%

19) 84 is what percent of 700? ___%

20) 40 is what percent of 500? __%

21) 26 is what percent of 100? __ %

22) 45 is what percent of 900? __%

23) 60 is what percent of 400? ____%

24) 18 is what percent of 900? ____%

25) 75 is what percent of 250? ____%

26) 27 is what percent of 900? ____%

27) 49 is what percent of 700? ____%

28) 81 is what percent of 900? ____%

29) 90 is what percent of 500? ____%

30) 82 is 20 percent of what number? ____

31) 14 is 35 percent of what number? ____

32) 90 is 6 percent of what number? ____

33) 80 is 40 percent of what number? ____

34) 90 is 15 percent of what number? ____

35) 28 is 7 percent of what number? ____

36) 54 is 18 percent of what number? ____

37) 72 is 24 percent of what number? ____

bit.ly/34Gy3FL

Find more at

Percent Problems - Answers

Solve each problem.

1) What is 5 percent of 300? 15

2) What is 15 percent of 600? 90

3) What is 12 percent of 450? 54

4) What is 30 percent of 240? 72

5) What is 60 percent of 850? 510

6) 63 is what percent of 300? 21%

7) 80 is what percent of 400? 20%

8) 70 is what percent of 700? 10%

9) 84 is what percent of 600? 14%

10) 90 is what percent of 300? 30%

11) 24 is what percent of 150? 16%

12) 12 is what percent of 80? 15%

13) 4 is what percent of 50? 8%

14) 110 is what percent of 500? 22%

15) 16 is what percent of 400? 4%

16) 39 is what percent of 300? 13%

17) 56 is what percent of 200? 28%

18) 30 is what percent of 500? 6%

19) 84 is what percent of 700? 12%

20) 40 is what percent of 500? 8%

21) 26 is what percent of 100? 26%

22) 45 is what percent of 900? 5%

23) 60 is what percent of 400? 15%

24) 18 is what percent of 900? 2%

25) 75 is what percent of 250? 30%

26) 27 is what percent of 900? 3%

27) 49 is what percent of 700? 7%

28) 81 is what percent of 900? 9%

29) 90 is what percent of 500? 18%

30) 82 is 20 percent of what number? 410

31) 14 is 35 percent of what number? 40

32) 90 is 6 percent of what number? 1,500

33) 80 is 40 percent of what number? 200

34) 90 is 15 percent of what number? 600

35) 28 is 7 percent of what number? 400

36) 54 is 18 percent of what number? 300

37) 72 is 24 percent of what number? 300

Percent of Increase and Decrease

✍ *Solve each percent of change word problem.*

1) Bob got a raise, and his hourly wage increased from $24 to $36. What is the

   percent increase? _____ %

2) The price of gasoline rose from $2.20 to $2.42 in one month. By what percent

   did the gas price rise? _____ %

3) In a class, the number of students has been increased from 30 to 39. What is

   the percent increase? _____ %

4) The price of a pair of shoes increases from $28 to $35. What is the percent

   increase? ____ %

5) In a class, the number of students has been decreased from 24 to 18. What is

   the percentage decrease? _____ %

6) Nick got a raise, and his hourly wage increased from $50 to $55. What is the

   percent increase? _____ %

7) A coat was originally priced at $80. It went on sale for $70.40. What was the

   percent that the coat was discounted? _____ %

8) The price of a pair of shoes increases from $8 to $12. What is the percent

   increase? ____ %

9) A house was purchased in 2002 for $180,000. It is now valued at $144,000.

   What is the rate (percent) of depreciation for the house?_____ %

10) The price of gasoline rose from $3.00 to $3.15 in one month. By

   what percent did the gas price rise? _____ %

bit.ly/3pgPQes

Find more at

Percent of Increase and Decrease - Answers

Solve each percent of change word problem.

1) Bob got a raise, and his hourly wage increased from $24 to $36. What is the percent increase? 50%

2) The price of gasoline rose from $2.20 to $2.42 in one month. By what percent did the gas price rise? 10%

3) In a class, the number of students has been increased from 30 to 39. What is the percent increase? 30%

4) The price of a pair of shoes increases from $28 to $35. What is the percent increase? 25%

5) In a class, the number of students has been decreased from 24 to 18. What is the percentage decrease? 25%

6) Nick got a raise, and his hourly wage increased from $50 to $55. What is the percent increase? 10%

7) A coat was originally priced at $80. It went on sale for $70.40. What was the percent that the coat was discounted? 12%

8) The price of a pair of shoes increases from $8 to $12. What is the percent increase? 50%

9) A house was purchased in 2002 for $180,000. It is now valued at $144,000. What is the rate (percent) of depreciation for the house? 20%

10) The price of gasoline rose from $3.00 to $3.15 in one month. By what percent did the gas price rise? 5%

bit.ly/3pgPQes
Find more at

Discount, Tax and Tip

✎ *Find the missing values.*

1) Original price of a computer: $400

   Tax: 5%, Selling price: $_____

2) Original price of a sofa: $600

   Tax: 12%, Selling price: $_____

3) Original price of a table: $550

   Tax: 18%, Selling price: $_____

4) Original price of a cell phone: $700

   Tax: 20%, Selling price: $_____

5) Original price of a printer: $400

   Tax: 22%, Selling price: $_____

6) Original price of a computer: $600

   Tax: 15%, Selling price: $_____

7) Restaurant bill: $24.00

   Tip: 25%, Final amount: $_____

8) Original price of a cell phone: $300

   Tax: 8%, Selling price: $_____

9) Original price of a carpet: $800

   Tax: 25%, Selling price: $_____

10) Original price of a camera: $200

    Discount: 35%, Selling price: $_____

11) Original price of a dress: $500

    Discount: 10%, Selling price: $_____

12) Original price of a monitor: $400

    Discount: 5%, Selling price: $_____

13) Original price of a laptop: $900

    Discount: 20%, Selling price: $_____

14) Restaurant bill: $54.00

    Tip: 20%, Final amount: $_____

Find more at bit.ly/2Je5lo0

Discount, Tax and Tip - Answers

Find the missing values.

1) Original price of a computer: $400

   Tax: 5%, Selling price: $420

2) Original price of a sofa: $600

   Tax: 12%, Selling price: $672

3) Original price of a table: $550

   Tax: 18%, Selling price: $649

4) Original price of a cell phone: $700

   Tax: 20%, Selling price: $840

5) Original price of a printer: $400

   Tax: 22%, Selling price: $488

6) Original price of a computer: $600

   Tax: 15%, Selling price: $690

7) Restaurant bill: $24.00

   Tip: 25%, Final amount: $30.00

8) Original price of a cell phone: $300

   Tax: 8%, Selling price: $324

9) Original price of a carpet: $800

   Tax: 25%, Selling price: $1,000

10) Original price of a camera: $200

    Discount: 35%, Selling price: $130

11) Original price of a dress: $500

    Discount: 10%, Selling price: $450

12) Original price of a monitor: $400

    Discount: 5%, Selling price: $380

13) Original price of a laptop: $900

    Discount: 20%, Selling price: $720

14) Restaurant bill: $54.00

    Tip: 20%, Final amount: $64.80

Simplifying Variable Expressions

✎ *Simplify and write the answer.*

1) $3x + 5 + 2x =$

2) $7x + 3 - 3x =$

3) $-2 - x^2 - 6x^2 =$

4) $(-6)(8x - 4) =$

5) $3 + 10x^2 + 2x =$

6) $8x^2 + 6x + 7x^2 =$

7) $2x^2 - 5x - 7x =$

8) $x - 3 + 5 - 3x =$

9) $2 - 3x + 12 - 2x =$

10) $5x^2 - 12x^2 + 8x =$

11) $2x^2 + 6x + 3x^2 =$

12) $2x^2 - 2x - x =$

13) $2x^2 - (-8x + 6) = 2$

14) $4x + 6(2 - 5x) =$

15) $10x + 8(10x - 6) =$

16) $9(-2x - 6) - 5 =$

17) $32x - 4 + 23 + 2x =$

18) $8x - 12x - x^2 + 13 =$

19) $(-6)(8x - 4) + 10x =$

20) $14x - 5(5 - 8x) =$

21) $23x + 4(9x + 3) + 12 =$

22) $3(-7x + 5) + 20x =$

23) $12x - 3x(x + 9) =$

24) $7x + 5x(3 - 3x) =$

25) $5x(-8x + 12) + 14x =$

26) $40x + 12 + 2x^2 =$

27) $5x(x - 3) - 10 =$

28) $8x - 7 + 8x + 2x^2 =$

29) $7x - 3x^2 - 5x^2 - 3 =$

30) $4 + x^2 - 6x^2 - 12x =$

31) $12x + 8x^2 + 2x + 20 =$

32) $23 + 15x^2 + 8x - 4x^2 =$

bit.ly/2WFVudQ

Find more at

Simplifying Variable Expressions - Answers

✎ *Simplify and write the answer.*

1) $3x + 5 + 2x = 5x + 5$

2) $7x + 3 - 3x = 4x + 3$

3) $-2 - x^2 - 6x^2 = -7x^2 - 2$

4) $(-6)(8x - 4) = -48x + 24$

5) $3 + 10x^2 + 2x = 10x^2 + 2x + 3$

6) $8x^2 + 6x + 7x^2 = 15x^2 + 6x$

7) $2x^2 - 5x - 7x = 2x^2 - 12x$

8) $x - 3 + 5 - 3x = -2x + 2$

9) $2 - 3x + 12 - 2x = -5x + 14$

10) $5x^2 - 12x^2 + 8x = -7x^2 + 8x$

11) $2x^2 + 6x + 3x^2 = 5x^2 + 6x$

12) $2x^2 - 2x - x = 2x^2 - 3x$

13) $2x^2 - (-8x + 6) = 2x^2 + 8x - 6$

14) $4x + 6(2 - 5x) = -26x + 12$

15) $10x + 8(10x - 6) = 90x - 48$

16) $9(-2x - 6) - 5 = -18x - 59$

17) $32x - 4 + 23 + 2x = 34x + 19$

18) $8x - 12x - x^2 + 13 = -x^2 - 4x + 13$

19) $(-6)(8x - 4) + 10x = -38x + 24$

20) $14x - 5(5 - 8x) = 54x - 25$

21) $23x + 4(9x + 3) + 12 = 59x + 24$

22) $3(-7x + 5) + 20x = -x + 15$

23) $12x - 3x(x + 9) = -3x^2 - 15x$

24) $7x + 5x(3 - 3x) = -15x^2 + 22x$

25) $5x(-8x + 12) + 14x = -40x^2 + 74x$

26) $40x + 12 + 2x^2 = 2x^2 + 40x + 12$

27) $5x(x - 3) - 10 = 5x^2 - 15x - 10$

28) $8x - 7 + 8x + 2x^2 = 2x^2 + 16x - 7$

29) $7x - 3x^2 - 5x^2 - 3 = -8x^2 + 7x - 3$

30) $4 + x^2 - 6x^2 - 12x = -5x^2 - 12x + 4$

31) $12x + 8x^2 + 2x + 20 = 8x^2 + 14x + 20$

32) $23 + 15x^2 + 8x - 4x^2 = 11x^2 + 8x + 23$

Simplifying Polynomial Expressions

✎ *Simplify and write the answer.*

1) $(2x^3 + 5x^2) - (12x + 2x^2) =$ _____

2) $(-x^5 + 2x^3) - (3x^3 + 6x^2) =$ _____

3) $(12x^4 + 4x^2) - (2x^2 - 6x^4) =$ _____

4) $4x - 3x^2 - 2(6x^2 + 6x^3) =$ _____

5) $(2x^3 - 3) + 3(2x^2 - 3x^3) =$ _____

6) $4(4x^3 - 2x) - (3x^3 - 2x^4) =$ _____

7) $2(4x - 3x^3) - 3(3x^3 + 4x^2) =$ _____

8) $(2x^2 - 2x) - (2x^3 + 5x^2) =$ _____

9) $2x^3 - (4x^4 + 2x) + x^2 =$ _____

10) $x^4 - 9(x^2 + x) - 5x =$ _____

11) $(-2x^2 - x^4) + (4x^4 - x^2) =$ _____

12) $4x^2 - 5x^3 + 15x^4 - 12x^3 =$ _____

13) $2x^2 - 5x^4 + 14x^4 - 11x^3 =$ _____

14) $2x^2 + 5x^3 - 7x^2 + 12x =$ _____

15) $2x^4 - 5x^5 + 8x^4 - 8x^2 =$ _____

16) $5x^3 + 17x - 5x^2 - 2x^3 =$ _____

bit.ly/2WT5gtn

Find more at

Simplifying Polynomial Expressions - Answers

✎ *Simplify and write the answer.*

1) $(2x^3 + 5x^2) - (12x + 2x^2) = 2x^3 + 3x^2 - 12x$

2) $(-x^5 + 2x^3) - (3x^3 + 6x^2) = -x^5 - x^3 - 6x^2$

3) $(12x^4 + 4x^2) - (2x^2 - 6x^4) = 18x^4 + 2x^2$

4) $4x - 3x^2 - 2(6x^2 + 6x^3) = -12x^3 - 15x^2 + 4x$

5) $(2x^3 - 3) + 3(2x^2 - 3x^3) = -7x^3 + 6x^2 - 3$

6) $4(4x^3 - 2x) - (3x^3 - 2x^4) = 2x^4 + 13x^3 - 8x$

7) $2(4x - 3x^3) - 3(3x^3 + 4x^2) = -15x^3 - 12x^2 + 8x$

8) $(2x^2 - 2x) - (2x^3 + 5x^2) = -2x^3 - 3x^2 - 2x$

9) $2x^3 - (4x^4 + 2x) + x^2 = -4x^4 + 2x^3 + x^2 - 2x$

10) $x^4 - 9(x^2 + x) - 5x = x^4 - 9x^2 - 14x$

11) $(-2x^2 - x^4) + (4x^4 - x^2) = 3x^4 - 3x^2$

12) $4x^2 - 5x^3 + 15x^4 - 12x^3 = 15x^4 - 17x^3 + 4x^2$

13) $2x^2 - 5x^4 + 14x^4 - 11x^3 = 9x^4 - 11x^3 + 2x^2$

14) $2x^2 + 5x^3 - 7x^2 + 12x = 5x^3 - 5x^2 + 12x$

15) $2x^4 - 5x^5 + 8x^4 - 8x^2 = -5x^5 + 10x^4 - 8x^2$

16) $5x^3 + 17x - 5x^2 - 2x^3 = 3x^3 - 5x^2 + 17x$

bit.ly/2WT5gtn

Find more at

Evaluating One Variable

✏️ *Evaluate each expression using the value given.*

1) $x = 3 \Rightarrow 6x - 9 =$

2) $x = 2 \Rightarrow 7x - 10 =$

3) $x = 1 \Rightarrow 5x + 2 =$

4) $x = 2 \Rightarrow 3x + 9 =$

5) $x = 4 \Rightarrow 4x - 8 =$

6) $x = 2 \Rightarrow 5x - 2x + 10 =$

7) $x = 3 \Rightarrow 2x - x - 6 =$

8) $x = 4 \Rightarrow 6x - 3x + 4 =$

9) $x = -2 \Rightarrow 4x - 6x - 5 =$

10) $x = -1 \Rightarrow 3x - 5x + 11 =$

11) $x = 1 \Rightarrow x - 7x + 12 =$

12) $x = 2 \Rightarrow 2(-3x + 4) =$

13) $x = 3 \Rightarrow 4(-5x - 2) =$

14) $x = 2 \Rightarrow 5(-2x - 4) =$

15) $x = -2 \Rightarrow 3(-4x - 5) =$

16) $x = 3 \Rightarrow 8x + 5 =$

17) $x = -3 \Rightarrow 12x + 9 =$

18) $x = -1 \Rightarrow 9x - 8 =$

19) $x = 2 \Rightarrow 16x - 10 =$

20) $x = 1 \Rightarrow 4x + 3 =$

21) $x = 5 \Rightarrow 7x - 2 =$

22) $x = 7 \Rightarrow 28 - x =$

23) $x = 3 \Rightarrow 5x - 10 =$

24) $x = 12 \Rightarrow 40 - 2x =$

25) $x = 2 \Rightarrow 11x - 2 =$

26) $x = 3 \Rightarrow 2x - x + 10 =$

bit.ly/3ppujQZ

Find more at

Evaluating One Variable - Answers

✏️ *Evaluate each expression using the value given.*

1) $x = 3 \Rightarrow 6x - 9 = 9$

2) $x = 2 \Rightarrow 7x - 10 = 4$

3) $x = 1 \Rightarrow 5x + 2 = 7$

4) $x = 2 \Rightarrow 3x + 9 = 15$

5) $x = 4 \Rightarrow 4x - 8 = 8$

6) $x = 2 \Rightarrow 5x - 2x + 10 = 16$

7) $x = 3 \Rightarrow 2x - x - 6 = -3$

8) $x = 4 \Rightarrow 6x - 3x + 4 = 16$

9) $x = -2 \Rightarrow 4x - 6x - 5 = -1$

10) $x = -1 \Rightarrow 3x - 5x + 11 = 13$

11) $x = 1 \Rightarrow x - 7x + 12 = 6$

12) $x = 2 \Rightarrow 2(-3x + 4) = -4$

13) $x = 3 \Rightarrow 4(-5x - 2) = -68$

14) $x = 2 \Rightarrow 5(-2x - 4) = -40$

15) $x = -2 \Rightarrow 3(-4x - 5) = 9$

16) $x = 3 \Rightarrow 8x + 5 = 29$

17) $x = -3 \Rightarrow 12x + 9 = -27$

18) $x = -1 \Rightarrow 9x - 8 = -17$

19) $x = 2 \Rightarrow 16x - 10 = 22$

20) $x = 1 \Rightarrow 4x + 3 = 7$

21) $x = 5 \Rightarrow 7x - 2 = 33$

22) $x = 7 \Rightarrow 28 - x = 21$

23) $x = 3 \Rightarrow 5x - 10 = 5$

24) $x = 12 \Rightarrow 40 - 2x = 16$

25) $x = 2 \Rightarrow 11x - 2 = 20$

26) $x = 3 \Rightarrow 2x - x + 10 = 13$

bit.ly/3ppujQZ

Find more at

Evaluating Two Variables

✎ *Evaluate each expression using the values given.*

1) $2x + 3y, x = 2, y = 3$

———

2) $3x + 4y, x = -1, y = -2$

———

3) $x + 6y, x = 3, y = 1$

———

4) $2a - (15 - b), a = 2, b = 3$

———

5) $4a - (6 - 3b), a = 1, b = 4$

———

6) $a - (8 - 2b), a = 2, b = 5$

———

7) $3z + 21 + 5k, z = 4, k = 1$

———

8) $-7a + 4b, a = 6, b = 3$

———

9) $-4a + 3b, a = 2, b = 4$

———

10) $-6a + 6b, a = 4, b = 3$

———

11) $-8a + 2b, a = 4, b = 6$

———

12) $4x + 6y, x = 6, y = 3$

———

13) $2x + 9y, x = 8, y = 1$

———

14) $x - 7y, x = 9, y = 4$

———

15) $5x - 4y, x = 6, y = 3$

———

16) $2z + 14 + 8k, z = 4, k = 1$

———

17) $6x + 3y, x = 3, y = 8$

———

18) $5a - 6b, a = -3, b = -1$

———

19) $8a + 4b, a = -4, b = 3$

———

20) $-2a - b, a = 4, b = 9$

———

21) $-7a + 3b, a = 4, b = 3$

———

22) $-5a + 9b, a = 7, b = 1$

———

bit.ly/2JfrzWJ

Find more at

Evaluating Two Variables - Answers

✎ *Evaluate each expression using the values given.*

1) $2x + 3y, x = 2, y = 3$
   13

2) $3x + 4y, x = -1, y = -2$
   -11

3) $x + 6y, x = 3, y = 1$
   9

4) $2a - (15 - b), a = 2, b = 3$
   -8

5) $4a - (6 - 3b), a = 1, b = 4$
   10

6) $a - (8 - 2b), a = 2, b = 5$
   4

7) $3z + 21 + 5k, z = 4, k = 1$
   38

8) $-7a + 4b, a = 6, b = 3$
   -30

9) $-4a + 3b, a = 2, b = 4$
   4

10) $-6a + 6b, a = 4, b = 3$
    -6

11) $-8a + 2b, a = 4, b = 6$
    -20

12) $4x + 6y, x = 6, y = 3$
    42

13) $2x + 9y, x = 8, y = 1$
    25

14) $x - 7y, x = 9, y = 4$
    -19

15) $5x - 4y, x = 6, y = 3$
    18

16) $2z + 14 + 8k, z = 4, k = 1$
    30

17) $6x + 3y, x = 3, y = 8$
    42

18) $5a - 6b, a = -3, b = -1$
    -9

19) $8a + 4b, a = -4, b = 3$
    -20

20) $-2a - b, a = 4, b = 9$
    -17

21) $-7a + 3b, a = 4, b = 3$
    -19

22) $-5a + 9b, a = 7, b = 1$
    -26

bit.ly/2JfrzWJ
Find more at

The Distributive Property

✎ *Use the distributive property to simply each expression.*

1) $(-3)(12x + 3) =$

2) $(-4x + 5)(-6) =$

3) $13(-4x + 2) =$

4) $7(6 - 3x) =$

5) $(6 - 5x)(-4) =$

6) $9(8 - 2x) =$

7) $(-4x + 6)5 =$

8) $(-2x + 7)(-8) =$

9) $8(-4x + 7) =$

10) $(-9x + 5)(-3) =$

11) $8(-x + 9) =$

12) $7(2 - 6x) =$

13) $(-12x + 4)(-3) =$

14) $(-6)(-10x + 6) =$

15) $(-5)(5 - 11x) =$

16) $9(4 - 8x) =$

17) $(-6x + 2)7 =$

18) $(-9)(1 - 12x) =$

19) $(-3)(4 - 6x) =$

20) $(2 - 8x)(-2) =$

21) $20(2 - x) =$

22) $12(-4x + 3) =$

23) $15(2 - 3x) =$

24) $(-4x + 5)2 =$

25) $(-11x + 8)(-2) =$

26) $14(5 - 8x) =$

bit.ly/38qCaXs

Find more at

The Distributive Property - Answers

✍️ *Use the distributive property to simply each expression.*

1) $(-3)(12x + 3) = -36x - 9$

2) $(-4x + 5)(-6) = 24x - 30$

3) $13(-4x + 2) = -52x + 26$

4) $7(6 - 3x) = -21x + 42$

5) $(6 - 5x)(-4) = 20x - 24$

6) $9(8 - 2x) = -18x + 72$

7) $(-4x + 6)5 = -20x + 30$

8) $(-2x + 7)(-8) = 16x - 56$

9) $8(-4x + 7) = -32x + 56$

10) $(-9x + 5)(-3) = 27x - 15$

11) $8(-x + 9) = -8x + 72$

12) $7(2 - 6x) = -42x + 14$

13) $(-12x + 4)(-3) = 36x - 12$

14) $(-6)(-10x + 6) = 60x - 36$

15) $(-5)(5 - 11x) = 55x - 25$

16) $9(4 - 8x) = -72x + 36$

17) $(-6x + 2)7 = -42x + 14$

18) $(-9)(1 - 12x) = 108x - 9$

19) $(-3)(4 - 6x) = 18x - 12$

20) $(2 - 8x)(-2) = 16x - 4$

21) $20(2 - x) = -20x + 40$

22) $12(-4x + 3) = -48x + 36$

23) $15(2 - 3x) = -45x + 30$

24) $(-4x + 5)2 = -8x + 10$

25) $(-11x + 8)(-2) = 22x - 16$

26) $14(5 - 8x) = -112x + 70$

bit.ly/38qCaXs

Find more at

One–Step Equations

✒️ *Solve each equation for x.*

1) $x - 15 = 24 \Rightarrow x = $ _____

2) $18 = -6 + x \Rightarrow x = $ ___

3) $19 - x = 8 \Rightarrow x = $ ___

4) $x - 22 = 24 \Rightarrow x = $ ___

5) $24 - x = 17 \Rightarrow x = $ ___

6) $16 - x = 3 \Rightarrow x = $ ___

7) $x - 14 = 12 \Rightarrow x = $ ___

8) $26 + x = 8 \Rightarrow x = $ ___

9) $x + 9 = -18 \Rightarrow x = $ ___

10) $x + 21 = 11 \Rightarrow x = $ ___

11) $17 = -5 + x \Rightarrow x = $ ___

12) $x + 20 = 29 \Rightarrow x = $ ___

13) $x - 13 = 19 \Rightarrow x = $ ___

14) $x + 9 = -17 \Rightarrow x = $ ___

15) $x - 4 = -23 \Rightarrow x = $ ___

16) $16 = -9 + x \Rightarrow x = $ ___

17) $4x = 28 \Rightarrow x = $ ___

18) $21 = -7x \Rightarrow x = $ ___

19) $12x = -12 \Rightarrow x = $ ___

20) $13x = 39 \Rightarrow x = $ ___

21) $8x = -16 \Rightarrow x = $ ___

22) $\frac{x}{2} = -5 \Rightarrow x = $ ___

23) $\frac{x}{9} = 6 \Rightarrow x = $ ___

24) $27 = \frac{x}{5} \Rightarrow x = $ ___

25) $\frac{x}{4} = -3 \Rightarrow x = $ ___

26) $x \div 8 = 7 \Rightarrow x = $ ___

27) $x \div 2 = -3 \Rightarrow x = $ ___

28) $4x = 48 \Rightarrow x = $ ___

29) $9x = 72 \Rightarrow x = $ ___

30) $8x = -32 \Rightarrow x = $ ___

31) $80 = -10x \Rightarrow x = $ ___

bit.ly/37Jq0tK

Find more at

One–Step Equations - Answers

✍ *Solve each equation for x.*

1) $x - 15 = 24 \Rightarrow x = 39$

2) $18 = -6 + x \Rightarrow x = 24$

3) $19 - x = 8 \Rightarrow x = 11$

4) $x - 22 = 24 \Rightarrow x = 46$

5) $24 - x = 17 \Rightarrow x = 7$

6) $16 - x = 3 \Rightarrow x = 13$

7) $x - 14 = 12 \Rightarrow x = 26$

8) $26 + x = 8 \Rightarrow x = -18$

9) $x + 9 = -18 \Rightarrow x = -27$

10) $x + 21 = 11 \Rightarrow x = -10$

11) $17 = -5 + x \Rightarrow x = 22$

12) $x + 20 = 29 \Rightarrow x = 9$

13) $x - 13 = 19 \Rightarrow x = 32$

14) $x + 9 = -17 \Rightarrow x = -26$

15) $x - 4 = -23 \Rightarrow x = -19$

16) $16 = -9 + x \Rightarrow x = 25$

17) $4x = 28 \Rightarrow x = 7$

18) $21 = -7x \Rightarrow x = -3$

19) $12x = -12 \Rightarrow x = -1$

20) $13x = 39 \Rightarrow x = 3$

21) $8x = -16 \Rightarrow x = -2$

22) $\frac{x}{2} = -5 \Rightarrow x = -10$

23) $\frac{x}{9} = 6 \Rightarrow x = 54$

24) $27 = \frac{x}{5} \Rightarrow x = 135$

25) $\frac{x}{4} = -3 \Rightarrow x = -12$

26) $x \div 8 = 7 \Rightarrow x = 56$

27) $x \div 2 = -3 \Rightarrow x = -6$

28) $4x = 48 \Rightarrow x = 12$

29) $9x = 72 \Rightarrow x = 8$

30) $8x = -32 \Rightarrow x = -4$

31) $80 = -10x \Rightarrow x = -8$

Multi –Step Equations

✎ *Solve each equation.*

1) $3x - 8 = 13 \Rightarrow x =$ _____

2) $23 = -(x - 5) \Rightarrow x =$ _____

3) $-(8 - x) = 15 \Rightarrow x =$ _____

4) $29 = -x + 12 \Rightarrow x =$ _____

5) $2(3 - 2x) = 10 \Rightarrow x =$ _____

6) $3x - 3 = 15 \Rightarrow x =$ _____

7) $32 = -x + 15 \Rightarrow x =$ _____

8) $-(10 - x) = -13 \Rightarrow x =$ _____

9) $-4(7 + x) = 4 \Rightarrow x =$ _____

10) $23 = 2x - 7 \Rightarrow x =$ _____

11) $-6(3 + x) = 6 \Rightarrow x =$ _____

12) $-3 = 3x - 15 \Rightarrow x =$ _____

13) $-7(12 + x) = 7 \Rightarrow x =$ _____

14) $8(6 - 4x) = 16 \Rightarrow x =$ _____

15) $18 - 4x = -9 - x \Rightarrow x =$ _____

16) $6(4 - x) = 30 \Rightarrow x =$ _____

17) $15 - 3x = -5 - x \Rightarrow x =$ _____

18) $9(-7 - 3x) = 18 \Rightarrow x =$ _____

19) $16 - 2x = -4 - 7x \Rightarrow x =$ _____

20) $14 - 2x = 14 + x \Rightarrow x =$ _____

21) $21 - 3x = -7 - 10x \Rightarrow x =$ _____

22) $8 - 2x = 11 + x \Rightarrow x =$ _____

23) $10 + 12x = -8 + 6x \Rightarrow x =$ _____

24) $25 + 20x = -5 + 5x \Rightarrow x =$ _____

25) $16 - x = -8 - 7x \Rightarrow x =$ _____

26) $17 - 3x = 13 + x \Rightarrow x =$ _____

27) $22 + 5x = -8 - x \Rightarrow x =$ _____

28) $-9(7 + x) = 9 \Rightarrow x =$ _____

29) $11 + 3x = -4 - 2x \Rightarrow x =$ _____

30) $13 - 2x = 3 - 3x \Rightarrow x =$ _____

31) $19 - x = -1 - 11x \Rightarrow x =$ _____

32) $12 - 2x = -2 - 4x \Rightarrow x =$ _____

bit.ly/3nQbSEB

Find more at

Multi –Step Equations - Answers

✎ *Solve each equation.*

1) $3x - 8 = 13 \Rightarrow x = 7$

2) $23 = -(x - 5) \Rightarrow x = -18$

3) $-(8 - x) = 15 \Rightarrow x = 23$

4) $29 = -x + 12 \Rightarrow x = -17$

5) $2(3 - 2x) = 10 \Rightarrow x = -1$

6) $3x - 3 = 15 \Rightarrow x = 6$

7) $32 = -x + 15 \Rightarrow x = -17$

8) $-(10 - x) = -13 \Rightarrow x = -3$

9) $-4(7 + x) = 4 \Rightarrow x = -8$

10) $23 = 2x - 7 \Rightarrow x = 15$

11) $-6(3 + x) = 6 \Rightarrow x = -4$

12) $-3 = 3x - 15 \Rightarrow x = 4$

13) $-7(12 + x) = 7 \Rightarrow x = -13$

14) $8(6 - 4x) = 16 \Rightarrow x = 1$

15) $18 - 4x = -9 - x \Rightarrow x = 9$

16) $6(4 - x) = 30 \Rightarrow x = -1$

17) $15 - 3x = -5 - x \Rightarrow x = 10$

18) $9(-7 - 3x) = 18 \Rightarrow x = -3$

19) $16 - 2x = -4 - 7x \Rightarrow x = -4$

20) $14 - 2x = 14 + x \Rightarrow x = 0$

21) $21 - 3x = -7 - 10x \Rightarrow x = -4$

22) $8 - 2x = 11 + x \Rightarrow x = -1$

23) $10 + 12x = -8 + 6x \Rightarrow x = -3$

24) $25 + 20x = -5 + 5x \Rightarrow x = -2$

25) $16 - x = -8 - 7x \Rightarrow x = -4$

26) $17 - 3x = 13 + x \Rightarrow x = 1$

27) $22 + 5x = -8 - x \Rightarrow x = -5$

28) $-9(7 + x) = 9 \Rightarrow x = -8$

29) $11 + 3x = -4 - 2x \Rightarrow x = -3$

30) $13 - 2x = 3 - 3x \Rightarrow x = -10$

31) $19 - x = -1 - 11x \Rightarrow x = -2$

32) $12 - 2x = -2 - 4x \Rightarrow x = -7$

bit.ly/3nQbSEB

Find more at

Graphing Single–Variable Inequalities

 Graph each inequality.

1) $x < 6$

2) $x \geq 1$

3) $x \geq -6$

4) $x \leq -2$

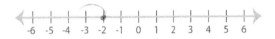

5) $x > -1$

6) $3 > x$

7) $2 \leq x$

8) $x > 0$

9) $-3 \leq x$

10) $-4 \leq x$

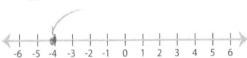

11) $x \leq 5$

12) $0 \leq x$

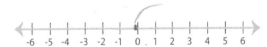

13) $-5 \leq x$

14) $x > -6$

bit.ly/3EQVUS6

Find more at

Graphing Single–Variable Inequalities - Answers

 Graph each inequality.

1) $x < 6$

2) $x \geq 1$

3) $x \geq -6$

4) $x \leq -2$

5) $x > -1$

6) $3 > x$

7) $2 \leq x$

8) $x > 0$

9) $-3 \leq x$

10) $-4 \leq x$

11) $x \leq 5$

12) $0 \leq x$

13) $-5 \leq x$

14) $x > -6$

bit.ly/3EQVUS6

Find more at

One–Step Inequalities

✍️ *Solve each inequality for x.*

1) $x - 10 < 22 \Rightarrow$ _____

2) $18 \leq -4 + x \Rightarrow$ _____

3) $x - 33 > 8 \Rightarrow$ _____

4) $x + 22 \geq 24 \Rightarrow$ _____

5) $x - 24 > 17 \Rightarrow$ _____

6) $x + 5 \geq 3 \Rightarrow x$_____

7) $x + 14 < 12 \Rightarrow$ _____

8) $26 + x \leq 8 \Rightarrow$ _____

9) $x + 9 \geq -18 \Rightarrow$ _____

10) $x + 24 < 11 \Rightarrow$ _____

11) $17 \leq -5 + x \Rightarrow$ _____

12) $x + 25 > 29 \Rightarrow x$_____

13) $x - 17 \geq 19 \Rightarrow$ _____

14) $x + 8 > -17 \Rightarrow$ _____

15) $x + 8 < -23 \Rightarrow$ _____

16) $16 \leq -5 + x \Rightarrow$ _____

17) $4x \leq 12 \Rightarrow$ _____

18) $28 \geq -7x \Rightarrow$ _____

19) $2x > -14 \Rightarrow$ _____

20) $13x \leq 39 \Rightarrow$ _____

21) $-8x > -16 \Rightarrow$ _____

22) $\frac{x}{2} < -6 \Rightarrow$ _____

23) $\frac{x}{6} > 6 \Rightarrow$ _____

24) $27 \leq \frac{x}{4} \Rightarrow$ _____

25) $\frac{x}{8} < -3 \Rightarrow$ _____

26) $6x \geq 18 \Rightarrow$ _____

27) $5x \geq -25 \Rightarrow$ _____

28) $4x > 48 \Rightarrow$ _____

29) $8x \leq 72 \Rightarrow$ _____

30) $-4x < -32 \Rightarrow$ _____

31) $40 > -10x \Rightarrow$ _____

Find more at
bit.ly/3rrEIgL

One–Step Inequalities - Answers

✍ *Solve each inequality for x.*

1) $x - 10 < 22 \Rightarrow x < 32$

2) $18 \leq -4 + x \Rightarrow 22 \leq x$

3) $x - 33 > 8 \Rightarrow 41 < x$

4) $x + 22 \geq 24 \Rightarrow x \geq 2$

5) $x - 24 > 17 \Rightarrow x > 41$

6) $x + 5 \geq 3 \Rightarrow x \geq -2$

7) $x + 14 < 12 \Rightarrow x < -2$

8) $26 + x \leq 8 \Rightarrow x \leq -18$

9) $x + 9 \geq -18 \Rightarrow x \geq -27$

10) $x + 24 < 11 \Rightarrow x < -13$

11) $17 \leq -5 + x \Rightarrow 22 \leq x$

12) $x + 25 > 29 \Rightarrow x > 4$

13) $x - 17 \geq 19 \Rightarrow x \geq 36$

14) $x + 8 > -17 \Rightarrow x > -25$

15) $x + 8 < -23 \Rightarrow x < -31$

16) $16 \leq -5 + x \Rightarrow 21 \leq x$

17) $4x \leq 12 \Rightarrow x \leq 3$

18) $28 \geq -7x \Rightarrow -4 \leq x$

19) $2x > -14 \Rightarrow x > -7$

20) $13x \leq 39 \Rightarrow x \leq 3$

21) $-8x > -16 \Rightarrow x < 2$

22) $\frac{x}{2} < -6 \Rightarrow x < -12$

23) $\frac{x}{6} > 6 \Rightarrow x > 36$

24) $27 \leq \frac{x}{4} \Rightarrow 108 \leq x$

25) $\frac{x}{8} < -3 \Rightarrow x < -24$

26) $6x \geq 18 \Rightarrow x \geq 3$

27) $5x \geq -25 \Rightarrow x \geq -5$

28) $4x > 48 \Rightarrow x > 12$

29) $8x \leq 72 \Rightarrow x \leq 9$

30) $-4x < -32 \Rightarrow x > 8$

31) $40 > -10x \Rightarrow -4 < x$

bit.ly/3rrEIgL

Find more at

Multi –Step Inequalities

✍ *Solve each inequality.*

1) $2x - 8 \leq 8 \rightarrow$ _____

2) $3 + 2x \geq 17 \rightarrow$ _____

3) $5 + 3x \geq 26 \rightarrow$ _____

4) $2x - 8 \leq 14 \rightarrow$ _____

5) $3x - 4 \leq 23 \rightarrow$ _____

6) $7x - 5 \leq 51 \rightarrow$ _____

7) $4x - 9 \leq 27 \rightarrow$ _____

8) $6x - 11 \leq 13 \rightarrow$ _____

9) $5x - 7 \leq 33 \rightarrow$ _____

10) $6 + 2x \geq 28 \rightarrow$ _____

11) $8 + 3x \geq 35 \rightarrow$ _____

12) $4 + 6x < 34 \rightarrow$ _____

13) $3 + 2x \geq 53 \rightarrow$ _____

14) $7 - 6x > 56 + x \rightarrow$ _____

15) $9 + 4x \geq 39 + 2x \rightarrow$ _____

16) $3 + 5x \geq 43 \rightarrow$ _____

17) $4 - 7x < 60 \rightarrow$ _____

18) $11 - 4x \geq 55 \rightarrow$ _____

19) $12 + x \geq 48 - 2x \rightarrow$ _____

20) $10 - 10x \leq -20 \rightarrow$ _____

21) $5 - 9x \geq -40 \rightarrow$ _____

22) $8 - 7x \geq 36 \rightarrow$ _____

23) $5 + 11x < 69 + 3x \rightarrow$ _____

24) $6 + 8x < 28 - 3x \rightarrow$ _____

25) $9 + 11x < 57 - x \rightarrow$ _____

26) $3 + 10x \geq 45 - 4x \rightarrow$ _____

Find more at bit.ly/2WK1xOr

Multi –Step Inequalities - Answers

🖎 *Solve each inequality.*

1) $2x - 8 \leq 8 \rightarrow x \leq 8$

2) $3 + 2x \geq 17 \rightarrow x \geq 7$

3) $5 + 3x \geq 26 \rightarrow x \geq 7$

4) $2x - 8 \leq 14 \rightarrow x \leq 11$

5) $3x - 4 \leq 23 \rightarrow x \leq 9$

6) $7x - 5 \leq 51 \rightarrow x \leq 8$

7) $4x - 9 \leq 27 \rightarrow x \leq 9$

8) $6x - 11 \leq 13 \rightarrow x \leq 4$

9) $5x - 7 \leq 33 \rightarrow x \leq 8$

10) $6 + 2x \geq 28 \rightarrow x \geq 11$

11) $8 + 3x \geq 35 \rightarrow x \geq 9$

12) $4 + 6x < 34 \rightarrow x < 5$

13) $3 + 2x \geq 53 \rightarrow x \geq 25$

14) $7 - 6x > 56 + x \rightarrow x < -7$

15) $9 + 4x \geq 39 + 2x \rightarrow x \geq 15$

16) $3 + 5x \geq 43 \rightarrow x \geq 8$

17) $4 - 7x < 60 \rightarrow x > -8$

18) $11 - 4x \geq 55 \rightarrow x \leq -11$

19) $12 + x \geq 48 - 2x \rightarrow x \geq 12$

20) $10 - 10x \leq -20 \rightarrow x \geq 3$

21) $5 - 9x \geq -40 \rightarrow x \leq 5$

22) $8 - 7x \geq 36 \rightarrow x \leq -4$

23) $5 + 11x < 69 + 3x \rightarrow x < 8$

24) $6 + 8x < 28 - 3x \rightarrow x < 2$

25) $9 + 11x < 57 - x \rightarrow x < 4$

26) $3 + 10x \geq 45 - 4x \rightarrow x \geq 3$

System of Equations

✏️ *Solve each system of equations.*

1) $-x + y = 2$　　　$x =$
　$-2x + y = 3$　　　$y =$

2) $-5x + y = -3$　　　$x =$
　$3x - 8y = 24$　　　$y =$

3) $y = -5$　　　$x =$
　$4x - 5y = 13$

4) $3y = -6x + 8$　　　$x =$
　$5x - 4y = -3$　　　$y =$

5) $10x - 8y = -15$　　$x =$
　$-6x + 4y = 13$　　　$y =$

6) $-3x - 4y = 5$　　　$x =$
　$x - 2y = 5$　　　$y =$

7) $5x - 12y = -19$　　$x =$
　$-6x + 7y = 8$　　　$y =$

8) $5x - 7y = -2$　　　$x =$
　$-x - 2y = -3$　　　$y =$

9) $-x + 3y = 3$　　　$x =$
　$-7x + 8y = -5$　　　$y =$

10) $-4x + 3y = -18$　　$x =$
　$4x - y = 14$　　　$y =$

11) $6x - 7y = -8$　　　$x =$
　$-x - 4y = -9$　　　$y =$

12) $-3x + 2y = -16$　　$x =$
　$4x - y = 13$　　　$y =$

bit.ly/3mPGO6k

System of Equations- Answers

✎ *Solve each system of equations.*

1) $-x + y = 2$ $x = -1$
   $-2x + y = 3$ $y = 1$

2) $-5x + y = -3$ $x = 0$
   $3x - 8y = 24$ $y = -3$

3) $y = -5$ $x = -3$
   $4x - 5y = 13$ $y = -5$

4) $y = -6x + 8$ $x = 1$
   $5x - 4y = -3$ $y = 2$

5) $10x - 8y = -15$ $x = -\dfrac{11}{2}$
   $-6x + 4y = 13$ $y = -5$

6) $-3x - 4y = 5$ $x = 1$
   $x - 2y = 5$ $y = -2$

7) $5x - 12y = -19$ $x = 1$
   $-6x + 7y = 8$ $y = 2$

8) $5x - 7y = -2$ $x = 1$
   $-x - 2y = -3$ $y = 1$

9) $-x + 3y = 3$ $x = 3$
   $-7x + 8y = -5$ $y = 2$

10) $-4x + 3y = -18$ $x = 3$
    $4x - y = 14$ $y = -2$

11) $6x - 7y = -8$ $x = 1$
    $-x - 4y = -9$ $y = 2$

12) $-3x + 2y = -16$ $x = 2$
    $4x - y = 13$ $y = -5$

Finding Slope

✎ *Find the slope of each line.*

1) $y = x - 5$, Slope $=$

2) $y = -3x + 2$, Slope $=$

3) $y = -x - 1$, Slope $=$

4) $y = -x - 9$, Slope $=$

5) $y = 5 + 2x$, Slope $=$

6) $y = 1 - 8x$, Slope $=$

7) $y = -4x + 3$, Slope $=$

8) $y = -9x + 8$, Slope $=$

9) $y = -2x + 4$, Slope $=$

10) $y = 9x - 8$, Slope $=$

11) $y = \frac{1}{2}x + 4$, Slope $=$

12) $y = -\frac{2}{5}x + 7$, Slope $=$

13) $-x + 3y = 5$, Slope $=$

14) $4x + 4y = 6$, Slope $=$

15) $6y - 2x = 10$, Slope $=$

16) $3y - x = 2$, Slope $=$

✎ *Find the slope of the line through each pair of points.*

1) $(4, 4), (8, 12)$, Slope $=$

7) $(8, 4), (9, 6)$, Slope $=$

2) $(-2, 4), (0, 6)$, Slope $=$

8) $(10, -1), (7, 8)$, Slope $=$

3) $(6, -2), (2, 6)$, Slope $=$

9) $(14, -7), (13, -6)$, Slope $=$

4) $(-4, -2), (0, 6)$, Slope $=$

10) $(10, 7), (8, 1)$, Slope $=$

5) $(6, 2), (3, 5)$, Slope $=$

11) $(5, 1), (8, 10)$, Slope $=$

6) $(-5, 1), (-1, 9)$, Slope $=$

1) $(9, -10), (8, 12)$, Slope $=$

bit.ly/3nMJYJv

Find more at

Finding Slope - Answers

✒️ *Find the slope of each line.*

1) $y = x - 5$, Slope $= 1$

2) $y = -3x + 2$, Slope $= -3$

3) $y = -x - 1$, Slope $= -1$

4) $y = -x - 9$, Slope $= -1$

5) $y = 5 + 2x$, Slope $= 2$

6) $y = 1 - 8x$, Slope $= -8$

7) $y = -4x + 3$, Slope $= -4$

8) $y = -9x + 8$, Slope $= -9$

9) $y = -2x + 4$, Slope $= -2$

10) $y = 9x - 8$, Slope $= 9$

11) $y = \frac{1}{2}x + 4$, Slope $= \frac{1}{2}$

12) $y = -\frac{2}{5}x + 7$, Slope $= -\frac{2}{5}$

13) $-x + 3y = 5$, Slope $= \frac{1}{3}$

14) $4x + 4y = 6$, Slope $= -1$

15) $6y - 2x = 10$, Slope $= \frac{1}{3}$

16) $3y - x = 2$, Slope $= \frac{1}{3}$

✒️ *Find the slope of the line through each pair of points.*

1) $(4, 4), (8, 12)$, Slope $= 2$

7) $(8, 4), (9, 6)$, Slope $= 2$

2) $(-2, 4), (0, 6)$, Slope $= 1$

8) $(10, -1), (7, 8)$, Slope $= -3$

3) $(6, -2), (2, 6)$, Slope $= -2$

9) $(14, -7), (13, -6)$, Slope $= -1$

4) $(-4, -2), (0, 6)$, Slope $= 2$

10) $(10, 7), (8, 1)$, Slope $= 3$

5) $(6, 2), (3, 5)$, Slope $= -1$

11) $(5, 1), (8, 10)$, Slope $= 3$

6) $(-5, 1), (-1, 9)$, Slope $= 2$

12) $(9, -10), (8, 12)$, Slope $= -22$

Graphing Lines Using Slope–Intercept Form

 Sketch the graph of each line.

1) $y = -x + 1$

2) $y = 2x - 3$

3) $y = -x + 2$

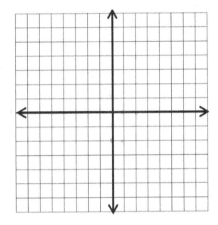 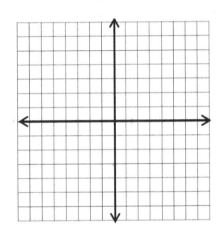 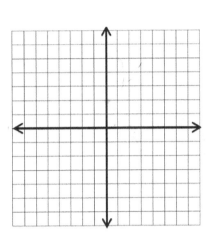

4) $y = x + 1$

5) $y = 2x - 4$

6) $y = -\frac{1}{2}x + 1$

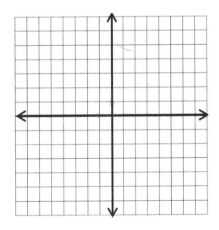 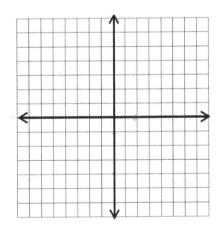 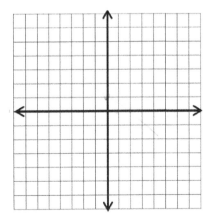

Find more at
bit.ly/3hfdnJL

Graphing Lines Using Slope–Intercept Form - Answers

✎ *Sketch the graph of each line.*

1) $y = -x + 1$

2) $y = 2x - 3$

3) $y = -x + 2$

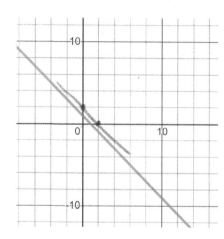

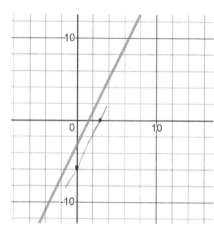

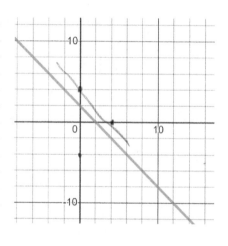

4) $y = x + 1$

5) $y = 2x - 4$

6) $y = -\frac{1}{2}x + 1$

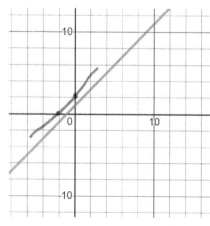

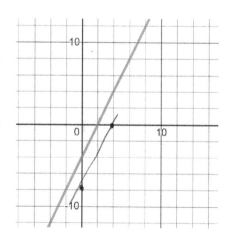

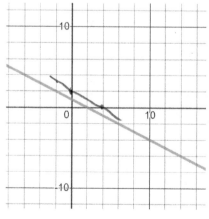

bit.ly/3hfdnJL

Find more at

Writing Linear Equations

✍ **Write the equation of the line through the given points.**

1) through: $(1, -2), (2, 4)$

$$y =$$

2) through: $(-2, 3), (1, 6)$

$$y =$$

3) through: $(-1, 2), (3, 6)$

$$y =$$

4) through: $(8, 5), (5, 2)$

$$y =$$

5) through: $(7, -10), (2, 10)$

$$y =$$

6) through: $(7, 2), (6, 1)$

$$y =$$

7) through: $(6, -1), (4, 1)$

$$y =$$

8) through: $(-2, 8), (-4, -6)$

$$y =$$

9) through: $(-2, 5), (-3, 4)$

$$y =$$

10) through: $(6, 8), (8, -6)$

$$y =$$

11) through: $(-2, 5), (-4, -3)$

$$y =$$

12) through: $(8, 8), (4, -8)$

$$y =$$

13) through: $(7, -4)$, Slope: -1

$$y =$$

14) through: $(4, -10)$, Slope: -2

$$y =$$

15) through: $(6, 10)$, Slope: 9

$$y =$$

16) through: $(-6, 8)$, Slope: -2

$$y =$$

✍ **Solve each problem.**

17) What is the equation of a line with slope 8 and intercept 5? _____

18) What is the equation of a line with slope 4 and intercept 10? _____

19) What is the equation of a line with slope 9 and passes through point $(5, 23)$?

_____ .

20) What is the equation of a line with slope -7 and passes through point $(-3, 18)$?

_____

bit.ly/3nMKcAl

Writing Linear Equations - Answers

✍ *Write the equation of the line through the given points.*

1) through: $(1, -2), (2, 4)$

$$y = 6x - 8$$

2) through: $(-2, 3), (1, 6)$

$$y = x + 5$$

3) through: $(-1, 2), (3, 6)$

$$y = x + 3$$

4) through: $(8, 5), (5, 2)$

$$y = x - 3$$

5) through: $(7, -10), (2, 10)$

$$y = -4x + 18$$

6) through: $(7, 2), (6, 1)$

$$y = x - 5$$

7) through: $(6, -1), (4, 1)$

$$y = -x + 5$$

8) through: $(-2, 8), (-4, -6)$

$$y = 7x + 22$$

9) through: $(-2, 5), (-3, 4)$

$$y = x + 7$$

10) through: $(6, 8), (8, -6)$

$$y = -7x + 50$$

11) through: $(-2, 5), (-4, -3)$

$$y = 4x + 13$$

12) through: $(8, 8), (4, -8)$

$$y = 4x - 24$$

13) through: $(7, -4)$, Slope: -1

$$y = -x + 3$$

14) through: $(4, -10)$, Slope: -2

$$y = -2x - 2$$

15) through: $(6, 10)$, Slope: 9

$$y = 9x - 44$$

16) through: $(-6, 8)$, Slope: -2

$$y = -2x - 4$$

✍ *Solve each problem.*

17) What is the equation of a line with slope 8 and intercept 5? $y = 8x + 5$

18) What is the equation of a line with slope 4 and intercept 10? $y = 4x + 10$

19) What is the equation of a line with slope 9 and passes through point $(5, 23)$?

$y = 9x - 22$

20) What is the equation of a line with slope -7 and passes through point $(-3, 18)$?

$$y = -7x - 3$$

Finding Midpoint

✍ *Find the midpoint of the line segment with the given endpoints.*

1) $(2, 2), (0, 4),$

   $midpoint = (\underline{\quad}, \underline{\quad})$

2) $(3, 3), (-1, 5),$

   $midpoint = (\underline{\quad}, \underline{\quad})$

3) $(2, -1), (0, 5),$

   $midpoint = (\underline{\quad}, \underline{\quad})$

4) $(-3, 7), (-1, 5),$

   $midpoint = (\underline{\quad}, \underline{\quad})$

5) $(5, -2), (9, -6),$

   $midpoint = (\underline{\quad}, \underline{\quad})$

6) $(-6, -3), (4, -7),$

   $midpoint = (\underline{\quad}, \underline{\quad})$

7) $(7, 0), (-7, 8),$

   $midpoint = (\underline{\quad}, \underline{\quad})$

8) $(-8, 4), (-4, 0),$

   $midpoint = (\underline{\quad}, \underline{\quad})$

9) $(-3, 6), (9, -8),$

   $midpoint = (\underline{\quad}, \underline{\quad})$

10) $(6, 8), (6, -6),$

   $midpoint = (\underline{\quad}, \underline{\quad})$

11) $(6, 7), (-8, 5),$

   $midpoint = (\underline{\quad}, \underline{\quad})$

12) $(9, 3), (-3, -9),$

   $midpoint = (\underline{\quad}, \underline{\quad})$

13) $(-6, 12), (-4, 6),$

   $midpoint = (\underline{\quad}, \underline{\quad})$

14) $(10, 7), (8, -3),$

   $midpoint = (\underline{\quad}, \underline{\quad})$

15) $(13, 7), (-5, 3),$

   $midpoint = (\underline{\quad}, \underline{\quad})$

16) $(-9, -4), (-5, 8),$

   $midpoint = (\underline{\quad}, \underline{\quad})$

17) $(11, 7), (5, 13),$

   $midpoint = (\underline{\quad}, \underline{\quad})$

18) $(-7, -10), (11, -2),$

   $midpoint = (\underline{\quad}, \underline{\quad})$

19) $(10, 15), (-4, 9),$

   $midpoint = (\underline{\quad}, \underline{\quad})$

20) $(11, -4), (7, 12),$

   $midpoint = (\underline{\quad}, \underline{\quad})$

Find more at
bit.ly/3nPdnTq

Finding Midpoint - Answers

 Find the midpoint of the line segment with the given endpoints.

1) $(2, 2), (0, 4),$
   $midpoint = (1, 3)$

2) $(3, 3), (-1, 5),$
   $midpoint = (1, 4)$

3) $(2, -1), (0, 5),$
   $midpoint = (1, 2)$

4) $(-3, 7), (-1, 5),$
   $midpoint = (-2, 6)$

5) $(5, -2), (9, -6),$
   $midpoint = (7, -4)$

6) $(-6, -3), (4, -7),$
   $midpoint = (-1, -5)$

7) $(7, 0), (-7, 8),$
   $midpoint = (0, 4)$

8) $(-8, 4), (-4, 0),$
   $midpoint = (-6, 2)$

9) $(-3, 6), (9, -8),$
   $midpoint = (3, -1)$

10) $(6, 8), (6, -6),$
    $midpoint = (6, 1)$

11) $(6, 7), (-8, 5),$
    $midpoint = (-1, 6)$

12) $(9, 3), (-3, -9),$
    $midpoint = (3, -3)$

13) $(-6, 12), (-4, 6),$
    $midpoint = (-5, 9)$

14) $(10, 7), (8, -3),$
    $midpoint = (9, 2)$

15) $(13, 7), (-5, 3),$
    $midpoint = (4, 5)$

16) $(-9, -4), (-5, 8),$
    $midpoint = (-7, 2)$

17) $(11, 7), (5, 13),$
    $midpoint = (8, 10)$

18) $(-7, -10), (11, -2),$
    $midpoint = (2, -6)$

19) $(10, 15), (-4, 9),$
    $midpoint = (3, 12)$

20) $(11, -4), (7, 12),$
    $midpoint = (9, 4)$

Finding Distance of Two Points

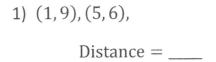 *Find the distance of each pair of points.*

1) $(1, 9), (5, 6),$

   Distance = ____

2) $(-4, 5), (8, 10),$

   Distance = ____

3) $(5, -2), (-3, 4),$

   Distance = ____

4) $(-3, 0), (3, 8),$

   Distance = ____

5) $(-5, 3), (4, -9),$

   Distance = ____

6) $(-7, -5), (5, 0),$

   Distance = ____

7) $(4, 3), (-4, -12),$

   Distance = ____

8) $(10, 1), (-5, -19),$

   Distance = ____

9) $(3, 3), (-1, 5),$

   Distance = ____

10) $(2, -1), (10, 5),$

    Distance = ____

11) $(3, 7), (-1, 4),$

    Distance = ____

12) $(5, -2), (9, -5),$

    Distance = ____

13) $(-8, 4), (4, 9),$

    Distance = ____

14) $(6, 8), (6, -6),$

    Distance = ____

15) $(9, 3), (-3, -2),$

    Distance = ____

16) $(-4, 12), (-4, 6),$

    Distance = ____

17) $(-9, -4), (-4, 8),$

    Distance = ____

18) $(11, 7), (3, 22),$

    Distance = ____

Find more at bit.ly/2KV50Hv

Finding Distance of Two Points - Answers

✎ *Find the distance of each pair of points.*

1) $(1, 9), (5, 6)$,

   Distance $= 5$

2) $(-4, 5), (8, 10)$,

   Distance $= 13$

3) $(5, -2), (-3, 4)$,

   Distance $= 10$

4) $(-3, 0), (3, 8)$,

   Distance $= 10$

5) $(-5, 3), (4, -9)$,

   Distance $= 15$

6) $(-7, -5), (5, 0)$,

   Distance $= 13$

7) $(4, 3), (-4, -12)$,

   Distance $= 17$

8) $(10, 1), (-5, -19)$,

   Distance $= 25$

9) $(3, 3), (-1, 5)$,

   Distance $= \sqrt{20} = 2\sqrt{5}$

10) $(2, -1), (10, 5)$,

    Distance $= 10$

11) $(3, 7), (-1, 4)$,

    Distance $= 5$

12) $(5, -2), (9, -5)$,

    Distance $= 5$

13) $(-8, 4), (4, 9)$,

    Distance $= 13$

14) $(6, 8), (6, -6)$,

    Distance $= 14$

15) $(9, 3), (-3, -2)$,

    Distance $= 13$

16) $(-4, 12), (-4, 6)$,

    Distance $= 6$

17) $(-9, -4), (-4, 8)$,

    Distance $= 13$

18) $(11, 7), (3, 22)$,

    Distance $= 17$

Multiplication Property of Exponents

✎ *Simplify and write the answer in exponential form.*

1) $2 \times 2^2 =$

2) $5^3 \times 5 =$

3) $3^2 \times 3^2 =$

4) $4^2 \times 4^2 =$

5) $7^3 \times 7^2 \times 7 =$

6) $2 \times 2^2 \times 2^2 =$

7) $5^3 \times 5^2 \times 5 \times 5 =$

8) $2x \times x =$

9) $x^3 \times x^2 =$

10) $x^4 \times x^4 =$

11) $x^2 \times x^2 \times x^2 =$

12) $6x \times 6x =$

13) $2x^2 \times 2x^2 =$

14) $3x^2 \times x =$

15) $4x^4 \times 4x^4 \times 4x^4 =$

16) $2x^2 \times x^2 =$

17) $x^4 \times 3x =$

18) $x \times 2x^2 =$

19) $5x^4 \times 5x^4 =$

20) $2yx^2 \times 2x =$

21) $3x^4 \times y^2x^4 =$

22) $y^2x^3 \times y^5x^2 =$

23) $4yx^3 \times 2x^2y^3 =$

24) $6x^2 \times 6x^3y^4 =$

25) $3x^4y^5 \times 7x^2y^3 =$

26) $7x^2y^5 \times 9xy^3 =$

27) $7xy^4 \times 4x^3y^3 =$

28) $3x^5y^3 \times 8x^2y^3 =$

29) $3x \times y^5x^3 \times y^4 =$

30) $yx^2 \times 2y^2x^2 \times 2xy =$

31) $4yx^4 \times 5y^5x \times xy^3 =$

32) $7x^2 \times 10x^3y^3 \times 8yx^4 =$

bit.ly/34AWHr1

Find more at

Multiplication Property of Exponents - Answers

✎ *Simplify and write the answer in exponential form.*

1) $2 \times 2^2 = 2^3$

2) $5^3 \times 5 = 5^4$

3) $3^2 \times 3^2 = 3^4$

4) $4^2 \times 4^2 = 4^4$

5) $7^3 \times 7^2 \times 7 = 7^6$

6) $2 \times 2^2 \times 2^2 = 2^5$

7) $5^3 \times 5^2 \times 5 \times 5 = 5^7$

8) $2x \times x = 2x^2$

9) $x^3 \times x^2 = x^5$

10) $x^4 \times x^4 = x^8$

11) $x^2 \times x^2 \times x^2 = x^6$

12) $6x \times 6x = 36x^2$

13) $2x^2 \times 2x^2 = 4x^4$

14) $3x^2 \times x = 3x^3$

15) $4x^4 \times 4x^4 \times 4x^4 = 64x^{12}$

16) $2x^2 \times x^2 = 2x^4$

17) $x^4 \times 3x = 3x^5$

18) $x \times 2x^2 = 2x^3$

19) $5x^4 \times 5x^4 = 25x^8$

20) $2yx^2 \times 2x = 4x^3y$

21) $3x^4 \times y^2x^4 = 3x^8y^2$

22) $y^2x^3 \times y^5x^2 = x^5y^7$

23) $4yx^3 \times 2x^2y^3 = 8x^5y^4$

24) $6x^2 \times 6x^3y^4 = 36x^5y^4$

25) $3x^4y^5 \times 7x^2y^3 = 21x^6y^8$

26) $7x^2y^5 \times 9xy^3 = 63x^3y^8$

27) $7xy^4 \times 4x^3y^3 = 28x^4y^7$

28) $3x^5y^3 \times 8x^2y^3 = 24x^7y^6$

29) $3x \times y^5x^3 \times y^4 = 3x^4y^9$

30) $yx^2 \times 2y^2x^2 \times 2xy = 4x^5y^4$

31) $4yx^4 \times 5y^5x \times xy^3 = 20x^6y^9$

32) $7x^2 \times 10x^3y^3 \times 8yx^4 = 560x^9y^4$

bit.ly/34AWHr1

Find more at

EffortlessMath.com

Division Property of Exponents

✎ *Simplify and write the answer.*

1) $\dfrac{2^2}{2^3} =$

2) $\dfrac{2^4}{2^2} =$

3) $\dfrac{5^5}{5} =$

4) $\dfrac{3}{3^5} =$

5) $\dfrac{x}{x^3} =$

6) $\dfrac{3 \times 3^3}{3^2 \times 3^4} =$

7) $\dfrac{5^8}{5^3} =$

8) $\dfrac{5 \times 5^6}{5^2 \times 5^7} =$

9) $\dfrac{3^4 \times 3^7}{3^2 \times 3^8} =$

10) $\dfrac{5x}{10x^3} =$

11) $\dfrac{5x^3}{2x^5} =$

12) $\dfrac{18x^3}{14x^6} =$

13) $\dfrac{12x^3}{8xy^8} =$

14) $\dfrac{24xy^3}{4x^4y^2} =$

15) $\dfrac{21x^3y^9}{7xy^5} =$

16) $\dfrac{36x^2y^9}{4x^3} =$

17) $\dfrac{12x^4y^4}{10x^6y^7} =$

18) $\dfrac{12y^2x^{12}}{20yx^8} =$

19) $\dfrac{16x^4y}{9x^8y^2} =$

20) $\dfrac{5x^8y^2}{20x^5y^5} =$

Find more at bit.ly/37JAclZ

Division Property of Exponents - Answers

✎ *Simplify and write the answer.*

1) $\dfrac{2^2}{2^3} = \dfrac{1}{2}$

2) $\dfrac{2^4}{2^2} = 2^2$

3) $\dfrac{5^5}{5} = 5^4$

4) $\dfrac{3}{3^5} = \dfrac{1}{3^4}$

5) $\dfrac{x}{x^3} = \dfrac{1}{x^2}$

6) $\dfrac{3^3}{3^4} = \dfrac{1}{3}$

7) $\dfrac{5^8}{5^3} = 5^5$

8) $\dfrac{5 \times 5^6}{5^2 \times 5^7} = \dfrac{1}{5^2}$

9) $\dfrac{3^4 \times 3^7}{3^2 \times 3^8} = 3$

10) $\dfrac{5x}{10x^3} = \dfrac{1}{2x^2}$

11) $\dfrac{5x^3}{2x^5} = \dfrac{5}{2x^2}$

12) $\dfrac{18x^3}{14x^6} = \dfrac{9}{7x^3}$

13) $\dfrac{12x^3}{8xy^8} = \dfrac{3x^2}{2y^8}$

14) $\dfrac{24xy^3}{4x^4y^2} = \dfrac{6y}{x^3}$

15) $\dfrac{21x^3y^9}{7xy^5} = 3x^2y^4$

16) $\dfrac{36x^2y^9}{4x^3} = \dfrac{9y^9}{x}$

17) $\dfrac{12x^4y^4}{10x^6y^7} = \dfrac{6}{5x^2y^3}$

18) $\dfrac{12y^2x^{12}}{20yx^8} = \dfrac{3yx^4}{5}$

19) $\dfrac{16x^4y}{9x^8y^2} = \dfrac{16}{9x^4y}$

20) $\dfrac{5x^8y^2}{20x^5y^5} = \dfrac{x^3}{4y^3}$

Powers of Products and Quotients

✍ *Simplify and write the answer.*

1) $(4^2)^2 =$

2) $(6^2)^3 =$

3) $(2 \times 2^3)^4 =$

4) $(4 \times 4^4)^2 =$

5) $(3^3 \times 3^2)^3 =$

6) $(5^4 \times 5^5)^2 =$

7) $(2 \times 2^4)^2 =$

8) $(2x^6)^2 =$

9) $(11x^5)^2 =$

10) $(4x^2y^4)^4 =$

11) $(2x^4y^4)^3 =$

12) $(3x^2y^2)^2 =$

13) $(3x^4y^3)^4 =$

14) $(2x^6y^8)^2 =$

15) $(12x^3x)^3 =$

16) $(5x^9x^6)^3 =$

17) $(5x^{10}y^3)^3 =$

18) $(14x^3x^3)^2 =$

19) $(3x^3 \times 5x)^2 =$

20) $(10x^{11}y^3)^2 =$

21) $(9x^7y^5)^2 =$

22) $(4x^4y^6)^5 =$

23) $(3x \cdot 4y^3)^2 =$

24) $\left(\frac{6x}{x^2}\right)^2 =$

25) $\left(\frac{x^5y^5}{x^2y^2}\right)^3 =$

26) $\left(\frac{24x}{4x^6}\right)^2 =$

27) $\left(\frac{x^5}{x^7y^2}\right)^2 =$

28) $\left(\frac{xy^2}{x^2y^3}\right)^3 =$

29) $\left(\frac{4xy^4}{x^5}\right)^2 =$

30) $\left(\frac{xy^4}{5xy^2}\right)^3 =$

Find more at bit.ly/34CgPJm

Powers of Products and Quotients - Answers

✎ *Simplify and write the answer.*

1) $(4^2)^2 = 4^4$

2) $(6^2)^3 = 6^6$

3) $(2 \times 2^3)^4 = 2^{16}$

4) $(4 \times 4^4)^2 = 4^{10}$

5) $(3^3 \times 3^2)^3 = 3^{15}$

6) $(5^4 \times 5^5)^2 = 5^{18}$

7) $(2 \times 2^4)^2 = 2^{10}$

8) $(2x^6)^2 = 4x^{12}$

9) $(11x^5)^2 = 121x^{10}$

10) $(4x^2y^4)^4 = 256x^8y^{16}$

11) $(2x^4y^4)^3 = 8x^{12}y^{12}$

12) $(3x^2y^2)^2 = 9x^4y^4$

13) $(3x^4y^3)^4 = 81x^{16}y^{12}$

14) $(2x^6y^8)^2 = 4x^{12}y^{16}$

15) $(12x^3x)^3 = 1,728x^{12}$

16) $(5x^9x^6)^3 = 125x^{45}$

17) $(5x^{10}y^3)^3 = 125x^{30}y^9$

18) $(14x^3x^3)^2 = 196x^{12}$

19) $(3x^3 \times 5x)^2 = 225x^8$

20) $(10x^{11}y^3)^2 = 100x^{22}y^6$

21) $(9x^7y^5)^2 = 81x^{14}y^{10}$

22) $(4x^4y^6)^5 = 1,024x^{20}y^{30}$

23) $(3x \times 4y^3)^2 = 144x^2y^6$

24) $\left(\frac{6x}{x^2}\right)^2 = \frac{36}{x^2}$

25) $\left(\frac{x^5y^5}{x^2y^2}\right)^3 = x^9y^9$

26) $\left(\frac{24x}{4x^6}\right)^2 = \frac{36}{x^{10}}$

27) $\left(\frac{x^5}{x^7y^2}\right)^2 = \frac{1}{x^4y^4}$

28) $\left(\frac{xy^2}{x^2y^3}\right)^3 = \frac{1}{x^3y^3}$

29) $\left(\frac{4xy^4}{x^5}\right)^2 = \frac{16y^8}{x^8}$

30) $\left(\frac{xy^4}{5xy^2}\right)^3 = \frac{y^6}{125}$

Zero and Negative Exponents

✎ *Evaluate the following expressions.*

1) $1^{-1} =$

2) $2^{-2} =$

3) $0^{15} =$

4) $1^{-10} =$

5) $8^{-1} =$

6) $8^{-2} =$

7) $2^{-4} =$

8) $10^{-2} =$

9) $9^{-2} =$

10) $3^{-3} =$

11) $7^{-3} =$

12) $3^{-4} =$

13) $6^{-3} =$

14) $5^{-3} =$

15) $22^{-1} =$

16) $4^{-4} =$

17) $5^{-4} =$

18) $15^{-2} =$

19) $4^{-5} =$

20) $9^{-3} =$

21) $3^{-5} =$

22) $5^{-4} =$

23) $12^{-3} =$

24) $15^{-3} =$

25) $20^{-3} =$

26) $50^{-2} =$

27) $18^{-3} =$

28) $24^{-2} =$

29) $30^{-3} =$

30) $10^{-5} =$

31) $\left(\frac{1}{8}\right)^{-1} =$

32) $\left(\frac{1}{5}\right)^{-2} =$

33) $\left(\frac{1}{7}\right)^{-2} =$

34) $\left(\frac{2}{3}\right)^{-2} =$

35) $\left(\frac{1}{5}\right)^{-3} =$

36) $\left(\frac{3}{4}\right)^{-2} =$

37) $\left(\frac{2}{5}\right)^{-2} =$

38) $\left(\frac{1}{2}\right)^{-8} =$

39) $\left(\frac{2}{5}\right)^{-3} =$

40) $\left(\frac{3}{7}\right)^{-2} =$

41) $\left(\frac{5}{6}\right)^{-3} =$

42) $\left(\frac{4}{9}\right)^{-2} =$

bit.ly/3rnkh4v

Find more at

Zero and Negative Exponents - Answers

✏️ *Evaluate the following expressions.*

1) $1^{-1} = 1$

2) $2^{-2} = \frac{1}{4}$

3) $0^{15} = 0$

4) $1^{-10} = 1$

5) $8^{-1} = \frac{1}{8}$

6) $8^{-2} = \frac{1}{64}$

7) $2^{-4} = \frac{1}{16}$

8) $10^{-2} = \frac{1}{100}$

9) $9^{-2} = \frac{1}{81}$

10) $3^{-3} = \frac{1}{27}$

11) $7^{-3} = \frac{1}{343}$

12) $3^{-4} = \frac{1}{81}$

13) $6^{-3} = \frac{1}{216}$

14) $5^{-3} = \frac{1}{125}$

15) $22^{-1} = \frac{1}{22}$

16) $4^{-4} = \frac{1}{256}$

17) $5^{-4} = \frac{1}{625}$

18) $15^{-2} = \frac{1}{225}$

19) $4^{-5} = \frac{1}{1,024}$

20) $9^{-3} = \frac{1}{729}$

21) $3^{-5} = \frac{1}{243}$

22) $5^{-4} = \frac{1}{625}$

23) $12^{-2} = \frac{1}{144}$

24) $15^{-3} = \frac{1}{3,375}$

25) $20^{-3} = \frac{1}{8,000}$

26) $50^{-2} = \frac{1}{2,500}$

27) $18^{-3} = \frac{1}{5,832}$

28) $24^{-2} = \frac{1}{576}$

29) $30^{-3} = \frac{1}{27,000}$

30) $10^{-5} = \frac{1}{100,000}$

31) $\left(\frac{1}{8}\right)^{-1} = 8$

32) $\left(\frac{1}{5}\right)^{-2} = 25$

33) $\left(\frac{1}{7}\right)^{-2} = 49$

34) $\left(\frac{2}{3}\right)^{-2} = \frac{9}{4}$

35) $\left(\frac{1}{5}\right)^{-3} = 125$

36) $\left(\frac{3}{4}\right)^{-2} = \frac{64}{27}$

37) $\left(\frac{2}{5}\right)^{-2} = \frac{25}{4}$

38) $\left(\frac{1}{2}\right)^{-8} = 256$

39) $\left(\frac{2}{5}\right)^{-3} = \frac{125}{8}$

40) $\left(\frac{3}{7}\right)^{-2} = \frac{49}{9}$

41) $\left(\frac{5}{6}\right)^{-3} = \frac{216}{125}$

42) $\left(\frac{4}{9}\right)^{-2} = \frac{81}{16}$

Negative Exponents and Negative Bases

✎ *Simplify and write the answer.*

1) $-3^{-1} =$

2) $-5^{-2} =$

3) $-2^{-4} =$

4) $-x^{-3} =$

5) $2x^{-1} =$

6) $-4x^{-3} =$

7) $-12x^{-5} =$

8) $-5x^{-2}y^{-3} =$

9) $20x^{-4}y^{-1} =$

10) $14a^{-6}b^{-7} =$

11) $-12x^2y^{-3} =$

12) $-\dfrac{25}{x^{-6}} =$

13) $-\dfrac{2x}{a^{-4}} =$

14) $\left(-\dfrac{1}{3x}\right)^{-2} =$

15) $\left(-\dfrac{3}{4x}\right)^{-2} =$

16) $-\dfrac{9}{a^{-7}b^{-2}} =$

17) $-\dfrac{5x}{x^{-3}} =$

18) $-\dfrac{a^{-3}}{b^{-2}} =$

19) $-\dfrac{8}{x^{-3}} =$

20) $\dfrac{5b}{-9c^{-4}} =$

21) $\dfrac{9ab}{a^{-3}b^{-1}} =$

22) $-\dfrac{15a^{-2}}{30b^{-3}} =$

23) $\dfrac{4ab^{-2}}{-3c^{-2}} =$

24) $\left(\dfrac{3a}{2c}\right)^{-2} =$

25) $\left(-\dfrac{5x}{3yz}\right)^{-3} =$

26) $\dfrac{11ab^{-2}}{-3c^{-2}} =$

27) $\left(-\dfrac{x^3}{x^4}\right)^{-2} =$

28) $\left(-\dfrac{x^{-2}}{3x^2}\right)^{-3} =$

bit.ly/3nPROSM

Find more at

Negative Exponents and Negative Bases - Answers

✍ *Simplify and write the answer.*

1) $-3^{-1} = -\frac{1}{3}$

2) $-5^{-2} = -\frac{1}{25}$

3) $-2^{-4} = -\frac{1}{16}$

4) $-x^{-3} = -\frac{1}{x^3}$

5) $2x^{-1} = \frac{2}{x}$

6) $-4x^{-3} = -\frac{4}{x^3}$

7) $-12x^{-5} = -\frac{12}{x^5}$

8) $-5x^{-2}y^{-3} = -\frac{5}{x^2y^3}$

9) $20x^{-4}y^{-1} = \frac{20}{x^4y}$

10) $14a^{-6}b^{-7} = \frac{14}{a^6b^7}$

11) $-12x^2y^{-3} = -\frac{12x^2}{y^3}$

12) $-\frac{25}{x^{-6}} = -25x^6$

13) $-\frac{2x}{a^{-4}} = -2xa^4$

14) $(-\frac{1}{3x})^{-2} = 9x^2$

15) $(-\frac{3}{4x})^{-2} = \frac{16x^2}{9}$

16) $-\frac{9}{a^{-7}b^{-2}} = -9a^7b^2$

17) $-\frac{5x}{x^{-3}} = -5x^4$

18) $-\frac{a^{-3}}{b^{-2}} = -\frac{b^2}{a^3}$

19) $-\frac{8}{x^{-3}} = -8x^3$

20) $\frac{5b}{-9c^{-4}} = -\frac{5bc^4}{9}$

21) $\frac{9ab}{a^{-3}b^{-1}} = 9a^4b^2$

22) $-\frac{15a^{-2}}{30b^{-3}} = -\frac{b^3}{2a^2}$

23) $\frac{4ab^{-2}}{-3c^{-2}} = -\frac{4ac^2}{3b^2}$

24) $(\frac{3a}{2c})^{-2} = \frac{4c^2}{9a^2}$

25) $(-\frac{5x}{3yz})^{-3} = -\frac{27y^3z^3}{125x^3}$

26) $\frac{11ab^{-2}}{-3c^{-2}} = -\frac{11ac^2}{3b^2}$

27) $(-\frac{x^3}{x^4})^{-2} = x^2$

28) $(-\frac{x^{-2}}{3x^2})^{-3} = -27x^{12}$

bit.ly/3nPROSM

Find more at

Scientific Notation

✎ *Write each number in scientific notation.*

1) $0.113 =$ 11) $2,000,000 =$

2) $0.02 =$ 12) $0.0000003 =$

3) $7.5 =$ 13) $554,000 =$

4) $20 =$ 14) $0.000725 =$

5) $60 =$ 15) $0.00034 =$

6) $0.004 =$ 16) $86,000,000 =$

7) $78 =$ 17) $62,000 =$

8) $1,600 =$ 18) $97,000,000 =$

9) $1,450 =$ 19) $0.0000045 =$

10) $31,000 =$ 20) $0.0019 =$

✎ *Write each number in standard notation.*

21) $2 \times 10^{-1} =$ 26) $9 \times 10^3 =$

22) $8 \times 10^{-2} =$ 27) $7 \times 10^5 =$

23) $1.8 \times 10^3 =$ 28) $1.15 \times 10^4 =$

24) $9 \times 10^{-4} =$ 29) $7 \times 10^{-5} =$

25) $1.7 \times 10^{-2} =$ 30) $8.3 \times 10^{-5} =$

Find more at
bit.ly/3nOwJYP

Scientific Notation - Answers

✏️ *Write each number in scientific notation.*

1) $0.113 = 1.13 \times 10^{-1}$

2) $0.02 = 2 \times 10^{-2}$

3) $7.5 = 2.5 \times 10^{0}$

4) $20 = 2 \times 10^{1}$

5) $60 = 6 \times 10^{1}$

6) $0.004 = 4 \times 10^{-3}$

7) $78 = 7.8 \times 10^{1}$

8) $1,600 = 1.6 \times 10^{3}$

9) $1,450 = 1.45 \times 10^{3}$

10) $31,000 = 3.1 \times 10^{4}$

11) $2,000,000 = 2 \times 10^{6}$

12) $0.0000003 = 3 \times 10^{-7}$

13) $554,000 = 5.54 \times 10^{5}$

14) $0.000725 = 7.25 \times 10^{-4}$

15) $0.00034 = 3.4 \times 10^{-4}$

16) $86,000,000 = 8.6 \times 10^{7}$

17) $62,000 = 6.2 \times 10^{4}$

18) $97,000,000 = 9.7 \times 10^{7}$

19) $0.0000045 = 4.5 \times 10^{-6}$

20) $0.0019 = 1.9 \times 10^{-3}$

✏️ *Write each number in standard notation.*

21) $2 \times 10^{-1} = 0.2$

22) $8 \times 10^{-2} = 0.08$

23) $1.8 \times 10^{3} = 1,800$

24) $9 \times 10^{-4} = 0.0009$

25) $1.7 \times 10^{-2} = 0.017$

26) $9 \times 10^{3} = 9,000$

27) $7 \times 10^{5} = 700,000$

28) $1.15 \times 10^{4} = 11,500$

29) $7 \times 10^{-5} = 0.00007$

30) $8.3 \times 10^{-5} = 0.000083$

Radicals

✍ *Simplify and write the answer.*

1) $\sqrt{0} =$ _____

2) $\sqrt{1} =$ _____

3) $\sqrt{4} =$ _____

4) $\sqrt{16} =$ _____

5) $\sqrt{9} =$ _____

6) $\sqrt{25} =$ _____

7) $\sqrt{49} =$ _____

8) $\sqrt{36} =$ _____

9) $\sqrt{64} =$ _____

10) $\sqrt{81} =$ _____

11) $\sqrt{121} =$ _____

12) $\sqrt{225} =$ _____

13) $\sqrt{144} =$ _____

14) $\sqrt{100} =$ _____

15) $\sqrt{256} =$ _____

16) $\sqrt{289} =$ _____

17) $\sqrt{324} =$ _____

18) $\sqrt{400} =$ _____

19) $\sqrt{900} =$ _____

20) $\sqrt{529} =$ _____

21) $\sqrt{361} =$ _____

22) $\sqrt{169} =$ _____

23) $\sqrt{196} =$ _____

24) $\sqrt{90} =$ _____

✍ *Evaluate.*

25) $\sqrt{6} \times \sqrt{6} =$

26) $\sqrt{5} \times \sqrt{5} =$

27) $\sqrt{8} \times \sqrt{8} =$

28) $\sqrt{2} + \sqrt{2} =$

29) $\sqrt{8} + \sqrt{8} =$

30) $6\sqrt{5} - 2\sqrt{5} =$

31) $\sqrt{25} \times \sqrt{16} =$

32) $\sqrt{25} \times \sqrt{64} =$

33) $\sqrt{81} \times \sqrt{25} =$

34) $5\sqrt{3} \times 2\sqrt{3} =$

35) $8\sqrt{2} \times 2\sqrt{2} =$

36) $6\sqrt{3} - \sqrt{12} =$

bit.ly/2WEATqr Find more at

Radicals - Answers

✍ *Simplify and write the answer.*

1) $\sqrt{0} = 0$

2) $\sqrt{1} = 1$

3) $\sqrt{4} = 2$

4) $\sqrt{16} = 4$

5) $\sqrt{9} = 3$

6) $\sqrt{25} = 5$

7) $\sqrt{49} = 7$

8) $\sqrt{36} = 6$

9) $\sqrt{64} = 8$

10) $\sqrt{81} = 9$

11) $\sqrt{121} = 11$

12) $\sqrt{225} = 15$

13) $\sqrt{144} = 12$

14) $\sqrt{100} = 10$

15) $\sqrt{256} = 16$

16) $\sqrt{289} = 17$

17) $\sqrt{324} = 18$

18) $\sqrt{400} = 20$

19) $\sqrt{900} = 30$

20) $\sqrt{529} = 23$

21) $\sqrt{361} = 19$

22) $\sqrt{169} = 13$

23) $\sqrt{196} = 14$

24) $\sqrt{90} = 3\sqrt{10}$

✍ *Evaluate.*

25) $\sqrt{6} \times \sqrt{6} = 6$

26) $\sqrt{5} \times \sqrt{5} = 5$

27) $\sqrt{8} \times \sqrt{8} = 8$

28) $\sqrt{2} + \sqrt{2} = 2\sqrt{2}$

29) $\sqrt{8} + \sqrt{8} = 2\sqrt{8} = 4\sqrt{2}$

30) $6\sqrt{5} - 2\sqrt{5} = 4\sqrt{5}$

31) $\sqrt{25} \times \sqrt{16} = 20$

32) $\sqrt{25} \times \sqrt{64} = 40$

33) $\sqrt{81} \times \sqrt{25} = 45$

34) $5\sqrt{3} \times 2\sqrt{3} = 30$

35) $8\sqrt{2} \times 2\sqrt{2} = 32$

36) $6\sqrt{3} - \sqrt{12} = 4\sqrt{3}$

bit.ly/2WEATqr

Find more at

Simplifying Polynomials

✎ *Simplify each expression.*

1) $2(2x + 2) =$

_____

2) $4(4x - 2) =$

_____

3) $3(5x + 3) =$

_____

4) $6(7x + 5) =$

_____

5) $-3(8x - 7) =$

_____

6) $2x(3x + 4) =$

_____

7) $3x^2 + 3x^2 - 2x^3 =$

_____

8) $2x - x^2 + 6x^3 + 4 =$

_____

9) $5x + 2x^2 - 9x^3 =$

_____

10) $7x^2 + 5x^4 - 2x^3 =$

_____

11) $-3x^2 + 5x^3 + 6x^4 =$

_____

12) $(x - 3)(x - 4) =$

_____

13) $(x - 5)(x + 4) =$

_____

14) $(x - 6)(x - 3) =$

_____

15) $(2x + 5)(x + 8) =$

_____

16) $(3x - 8)(x + 4) =$

_____

17) $-8x^2 + 2x^3 - 10x^4 + 5x =$

_____

18) $11 - 6x^2 + 5x^2 - 12x^3 + 22 =$

_____

19) $2x^2 - 2x + 3x^3 + 12x - 22x =$

_____

20) $11 - 4x^2 + 3x^2 - 7x^3 + 3 =$

_____

21) $2x^5 - x^3 + 8x^2 - 2x^5 =$

_____

22) $(2x^3 - 1) + (3x^3 - 2x^3) =$

_____

bit.ly/3rnAcj8

Find more at

Simplifying Polynomials - Answers

✎ **Simplify each expression.**

1) $2(2x + 2) =$

$4x + 4$

2) $4(4x - 2) =$

$16x - 8$

3) $3(5x + 3) =$

$15x + 9$

4) $6(7x + 5) =$

$42x + 30$

5) $-3(8x - 7) =$

$-24x + 21$

6) $2x(3x + 4) =$

$6x^2 + 8x$

7) $3x^2 + 3x^2 - 2x^3 =$

$-2x^3 + 6x^2$

8) $2x - x^2 + 6x^3 + 4 =$

$6x^3 - x^2 + 2x + 4$

9) $5x + 2x^2 - 9x^3 =$

$-9x^3 + 2x^2 + 5x$

10) $7x^2 + 5x^4 - 2x^3 =$

$5x^4 - 2x^3 + 7x^2$

11) $-3x^2 + 5x^3 + 6x^4 =$

$6x^4 + 5x^3 - 3x^2$

12) $(x - 3)(x - 4) =$

$x^2 - 7x + 12$

13) $(x - 5)(x + 4) =$

$x^2 - x - 20$

14) $(x - 6)(x - 3) =$

$x^2 - 9x + 18$

15) $(2x + 5)(x + 8) =$

$2x^2 + 21x + 40$

16) $(3x - 8)(x + 4) =$

$3x^2 + 4x - 32$

17) $-8x^2 + 2x^3 - 10x^4 + 5x =$

$-10x^4 + 2x^3 - 8x^2 + 5x$

18) $11 - 6x^2 + 5x^2 - 12x^3 + 22 =$

$-12x^3 - x^2 + 33$

19) $2x^2 - 2x + 3x^3 + 12x - 22x =$

$3x^3 + 2x^2 - 12x$

20) $11 - 4x^2 + 3x^2 - 7x^3 + 3 =$

$-7x^3 - x^2 + 14$

21) $2x^5 - x^3 + 8x^2 - 2x^5 =$

$-x^3 + 8x^2$

22) $(2x^3 - 1) + (3x^3 - 2x^3) =$

$3x^3 - 1$

bit.ly/3rnAcj8

Find more at

Adding and Subtracting Polynomials

✎ *Add or subtract expressions.*

1) $(x^2 - 3) + (x^2 + 1) =$

_____

2) $(2x^2 - 4) - (2 - 4x^2) =$

_____

3) $(x^3 + 2x^2) - (x^3 + 5) =$

_____

4) $(3x^3 - x^2) + (4x^2 - 7x) =$

_____

5) $(2x^3 + 3x) - (5x^3 + 2) =$

_____

6) $(5x^3 - 2) + (2x^3 + 10) =$

_____

7) $(7x^3 + 5) - (9 - 4x^3) =$

_____

8) $(5x^2 + 3x^3) - (2x^3 + 6) =$

_____

9) $(8x^2 - x) + (4x - 8x^2) =$

_____

10) $(6x + 9x^2) - (5x + 2) =$

_____

11) $(7x^4 - 2x) - (6x - 2x^4) =$

_____

12) $(2x - 4x^3) - (9x^3 + 6x) =$

_____

13) $(8x^3 - 8x^2) - (6x^2 - 3x) =$

_____

14) $(9x^2 - 6) + (5x^2 - 4x^3) =$

_____

15) $(8x^3 + 3x^4) - (x^4 - 3x^3) =$

_____

16) $(-4x^3 - 2x) + (5x - 2x^3) =$

_____

17) $(6x - 4x^4) - (8x^4 + 3x) =$

_____

18) $(7x - 8x^2) - (9x^4 - 3x^2) =$

_____

19) $(9x^3 - 6) + (9x^3 - 5x^2) =$

_____

20) $(5x^3 + x^4) - (8x^4 - 7x^3) =$

_____

bit.ly/2KUqHqQ

Find more at

Adding and Subtracting Polynomials - Answers

✎ *Add or subtract expressions.*

1) $(x^2 - 3) + (x^2 + 1) =$

$2x^2 - 2$

2) $(2x^2 - 4) - (2 - 4x^2) =$

$6x^2 - 6$

3) $(x^3 + 2x^2) - (x^3 + 5) =$

$2x^2 - 5$

4) $(3x^3 - x^2) + (4x^2 - 7x) =$

$3x^3 + 3x^2 - 7x$

5) $(2x^3 + 3x) - (5x^3 + 2) =$

$-3x^3 + 3x - 2$

6) $(5x^3 - 2) + (2x^3 + 10) =$

$7x^3 + 8$

7) $(7x^3 + 5) - (9 - 4x^3) =$

$11x^3 - 4$

8) $(5x^2 + 3x^3) - (2x^3 + 6) =$

$x^3 + 5x^2 - 6$

9) $(8x^2 - x) + (4x - 8x^2) =$

$3x$

10) $(6x + 9x^2) - (5x + 2) =$

$9x^2 + x - 2$

11) $(7x^4 - 2x) - (6x - 2x^4) =$

$9x^4 - 8x$

12) $(2x - 4x^3) - (9x^3 + 6x) =$

$-13x^3 - 4x$

13) $(8x^3 - 8x^2) - (6x^2 - 3x) =$

$8x^3 - 14x^2 + 3x$

14) $(9x^2 - 6) + (5x^2 - 4x^3) =$

$-4x^3 + 14x^2 - 6$

15) $(8x^3 + 3x^4) - (x^4 - 3x^3) =$

$2x^4 + 11x^3$

16) $(-4x^3 - 2x) + (5x - 2x^3) =$

$-6x^3 + 3x$

17) $(6x - 4x^4) - (8x^4 + 3x) =$

$-12x^4 + 3x$

18) $(7x - 8x^2) - (9x^4 - 3x^2) =$

$-9x^4 - 5x^2 + 7x$

19) $(9x^3 - 6) + (9x^3 - 5x^2) =$

$18x^3 - 5x^2 - 6$

20) $(5x^3 + x^4) - (8x^4 - 7x^3) =$

$-7x^4 + 12x^3$

Multiplying Monomials

✑ *Simplify each expression.*

1) $5x^8 \times x^3 =$

_____

2) $5y^5 \times 6y^3 =$

_____

3) $-4z^7 \times 5z^5 =$

_____

4) $7x^5y \times 3xy^2 =$

_____

5) $-6xy^8 \times 3x^5y^3 =$

_____

6) $7a^4b^2 \times 3a^8b =$

_____

7) $5xy^5 \times 3x^3y^4 =$

_____

8) $5p^5q^4 \times (-6pq^4) =$

_____

9) $8s^6t^2 \times 6s^3t^7 =$

_____

10) $(-8x^5y^2) \times 4x^6y^3 =$

_____

11) $9xy^6z \times 3y^4z^2 =$

_____

12) $12x^5y^4 \times 2x^8y =$

_____

13) $4pq^5 \times (-7p^4q^8) =$

_____

14) $9s^4t^2 \times (-5st^5) =$

_____

15) $10p^3q^5 \times (-4p^4q^6) =$

_____

16) $(-5p^2q^4r) \times 7pq^5r^3 =$

_____

17) $(-9a^4b^7c^4) \times (-4a^7b) =$

_____

18) $7u^5v^9 \times (-5u^{12}v^7) =$

_____

19) $5u^3v^9z^2 \times (-4uv^9z) =$

_____

20) $(-9xy^2z^4) \times 2x^2yz^5 =$

_____

21) $8x^3y^2z^5 \times (-9x^4y^2z) =$

_____

22) $6a^8b^8c^{12} \times 9a^7b^5c^8 =$

_____

bit.ly/2KLVoP8

Find more at

Multiplying Monomials - Answers

✎ *Simplify each expression.*

1) $5x^8 \times x^3 =$

$5x^{11}$

2) $5y^5 \times 6y^3 =$

$30y^8$

3) $-4z^7 \times 5z^5 =$

$-20z^{12}$

4) $7x^5y \times 3xy^2 =$

$21x^6y^3$

5) $-6xy^8 \times 3x^5y^3 =$

$-18x^6y^{11}$

6) $7a^4b^2 \times 3a^8b =$
$21a^{12}b^3$

7) $5xy^5 \times 3x^3y^4 =$

$15x^4y^9$

8) $5p^5q^4 \times (-6pq^4) =$

$-30p^6q^8$

9) $8s^6t^2 \times 6s^3t^7 =$

$48s^9t^9$

10) $(-8x^5y^2) \times 4x^6y^3 =$

$-32x^{11}y^5$

11) $9xy^6z \times 3y^4z^2 =$

$27xy^{10}z^3$

12) $12x^5y^4 \times 2x^8y =$

$24x^{13}y^5$

13) $4pq^5 \times (-7p^4q^8) =$

$-28p^5q^{13}$

14) $9s^4t^2 \times (-5st^5) =$

$-45s^5t^7$

15) $10p^3q^5 \times (-4p^4q^6) =$

$-40p^7q^{11}$

16) $(-5p^2q^4r) \times 7pq^5r^3 =$

$-35p^3q^9r^4$

17) $(-9a^4b^7c^4) \times (-4a^7b) =$

$36a^{11}b^8c^4$

18) $7u^5v^9 \times (-5u^{12}v^7) =$

$-35u^{17}v^{16}$

19) $5u^3v^9z^2 \times (-4uv^9z) =$

$-20u^4v^{18}z^3$

20) $(-9xy^2z^4) \times 2x^2yz^5 =$

$-18x^3y^3z^9$

21) $8x^3y^2z^5 \times (-9x^4y^2z) =$

$-72x^7y^4z^6$

22) $6a^8b^8c^{12} \times 9a^7b^5c^8 =$

$54a^{15}b^{13}c^{20}$

Multiplying and Dividing Monomials

✍ *Simplify each expression.*

1) $(8x^3)(2x^2) =$

_____

2) $(4x^6)(5x^4) =$

_____

3) $(-6x^8)(3x^3) =$

_____

4) $(5x^8y^9)(-6x^6y^9) =$

_____

5) $(8x^5y^6)(3x^2y^5) =$

_____

6) $(8yx^2)(7y^5x^3) =$

_____

7) $(4x^2y)(2x^2y^3) =$

_____

8) $(-2x^9y^4)(-9x^6y^8) =$

_____

9) $(-5x^8y^2)(-6x^4y^5) =$

_____

10) $(8x^8y)(-7x^4y^3) =$

_____

11) $(9x^6y^2)(6x^7y^4) =$

_____

12) $(8x^9y^5)(6x^5y^4) =$

_____

13) $(-5x^8y^9)(7x^7y^8) =$

_____

14) $(6x^2y^5)(5x^3y^2) =$

_____

15) $(9x^5y^{12})(4x^7y^9) =$

_____

16) $(-10x^{14}y^8)(2x^7y^5) =$

_____

17) $\dfrac{8x^4y^3}{xy^2} =$

_____

18) $\dfrac{6x^5y^6}{2x^3y} =$

_____

19) $\dfrac{12x^3y^7}{4xy} =$

_____

20) $\dfrac{-20x^8y^9}{5x^5y^4} =$

_____

bit.ly/2WHp4Q4

Find more at

Multiplying and Dividing Monomials - Answers

✎ *Simplify each expression.*

1) $(8x^3)(2x^2) =$

$16x^5$

2) $(4x^6)(5x^4) =$

$20x^{10}$

3) $(-6x^8)(3x^3) =$

$-18x^{11}$

4) $(5x^8y^9)(-6x^6y^9) =$

$-30x^{14}y^{18}$

5) $(8x^5y^6)(3x^2y^5) =$

$24x^7y^{11}$

6) $(8yx^2)(7y^5x^3) =$

$56y^6x^5$

7) $(4x^2y)(2x^2y^3) =$

$8x^4y^4$

8) $(-2x^9y^4)(-9x^6y^8) =$

$18x^{15}y^{12}$

9) $(-5x^8y^2)(-6x^4y^5) =$

$30x^{12}y^7$

10) $(8x^8y)(-7x^4y^3) =$

$-56x^{12}y^4$

11) $(9x^6y^2)(6x^7y^4) =$

$54x^{13}y^6$

12) $(8x^9y^5)(6x^5y^4) =$

$48x^{14}y^9$

13) $(-5x^8y^9)(7x^7y^8) =$

$-35x^{15}y^{17}$

14) $(6x^2y^5)(5x^3y^2) =$

$30x^5y^7$

15) $(9x^5y^{12})(4x^7y^9) =$

$36x^{12}y^{21}$

16) $(-10x^{14}y^8)(2x^7y^5) =$

$-20x^{21}y^{13}$

17) $\dfrac{8x^4y^3}{xy^2} =$

$8x^3y$

18) $\dfrac{6x^5y^6}{2x^3y} =$

$3x^2y^5$

19) $\dfrac{12x^3y^7}{4xy} =$

$3x^2y^6$

20) $\dfrac{-20x^8y^9}{5x^5y^4} =$

$-4x^3y^5$

bit.ly/2WHp4Q4

Find more at

Multiplying a Polynomial and a Monomial

✎ *Find each product.*

1) $x(x-2) =$

_____

2) $2(2+x) =$

_____

3) $x(x-1) =$

_____

4) $x(x+3) =$

_____

5) $2x(x-2) =$

_____

6) $5(4x+3) =$

_____

7) $4x(3x-4) =$

_____

8) $x(5x+2y) =$

_____

9) $3x(x-2y) =$

_____

10) $6x(3x-4y) =$

_____

11) $2x(3x-8) =$

_____

12) $6x(4x-6y) =$

_____

13) $3x(4x-2y) =$

_____

14) $2x(2x-6y) =$

_____

15) $5x(x^2+y^2) =$

_____

16) $3x(2x^2-y^2) =$

_____

17) $7(2x^2+9y^2) =$

_____

18) $2x(-2x^2y+3y) =$

_____

19) $-2(2x^2-4xy+2) =$

_____

20) $5(x^2-6xy-8) =$

_____

bit.ly/3aBYdx2

Find more at

Multiplying a Polynomial and a Monomial - Answers

✎ *Find each product.*

1) $x(x-2) =$

$x^2 - 2x$

2) $2(2+x) =$

$2x + 4$

3) $x(x-1) =$

$x^2 - x$

4) $x(x+3) =$

$x^2 + 3x$

5) $2x(x-2) =$

$2x^2 - 4x$

6) $5(4x+3) =$

$20x + 15$

7) $4x(3x-4) =$

$12x^2 - 16x$

8) $x(5x+2y) =$

$5x^2 + 2xy$

9) $3x(x-2y) =$

$3x^2 - 6xy$

10) $6x(3x-4y) =$

$18x^2 - 24xy$

11) $2x(3x-8) =$

$6x^2 - 16x$

12) $6x(4x-6y) =$

$24x^2 - 36xy$

13) $3x(4x-2y) =$

$12x^2 - 6xy$

14) $2x(2x-6y) =$

$4x^2 - 12xy$

15) $5x(x^2+y^2) =$

$5x^3 - 5xy^2$

16) $3x(2x^2-y^2) =$

$6x^3 - 3xy^2$

17) $7(2x^2+9y^2) =$

$14x^3 + 63y^2$

18) $2x(-2x^2y+3y) =$

$-4x^3y + 6xy$

19) $-2(2x^2-4xy+2) =$

$-4x^2 + 8xy - 4$

20) $5(x^2-6xy-8) =$

$5x^2 - 30xy - 40$

Multiplying Binomials

✎ *Find each product.*

1) $(x - 2)(x + 5) =$

_____

2) $(x + 4)(x + 2) =$

_____

3) $(x - 2)(x - 4) =$

_____

4) $(x - 8)(x - 2) =$

_____

5) $(x - 7)(x - 5) =$

_____

6) $(x + 6)(x + 2) =$

_____

7) $(x - 9)(x + 3) =$

_____

8) $(x - 8)(x - 5) =$

_____

9) $(x + 3)(x + 7) =$

_____

10) $(x - 9)(x + 4) =$

_____

11) $(x + 6)(x + 6) =$

_____

12) $(x + 7)(x + 7) =$

_____

13) $(x - 8)(x + 7) =$

_____

14) $(x + 9)(x + 9) =$

_____

15) $(x - 8)(x - 8) =$

_____

16) $(2x - 9)(x + 5) =$

_____

17) $(2x - 3)(x + 4) =$

_____

18) $(2x + 4)(x + 2) =$

_____

19) $(2x + 2)(x + 3) =$

_____

20) $(2x - 4)(2x + 2) =$

_____

bit.ly/3aCs0FL

Find more at

Multiplying Binomials - Answers

✏️ *Find each product.*

1) $(x - 2)(x + 5) =$

$x^2 + 3x - 10$

2) $(x + 4)(x + 2) =$

$x^2 + 6x + 8$

3) $(x - 2)(x - 4) =$

$x^2 - 6x + 8$

4) $(x - 8)(x - 2) =$

$x^2 - 10x + 16$

5) $(x - 7)(x - 5) =$

$x^2 - 12x + 35$

6) $(x + 6)(x + 2) =$

$x^2 + 8x + 12$

7) $(x - 9)(x + 3) =$

$x^2 - 6x - 27$

8) $(x - 8)(x - 5) =$

$x^2 - 13x + 40$

9) $(x + 3)(x + 7) =$

$x^2 + 10x + 21$

10) $(x - 9)(x + 4) =$

$x^2 - 5x - 36$

11) $(x + 6)(x + 6) =$

$x^2 + 12x + 36$

12) $(x + 7)(x + 7) =$

$x^2 + 14x + 49$

13) $(x - 8)(x + 7) =$

$x^2 - x - 56$

14) $(x + 9)(x + 9) =$

$x^2 + 18x + 81$

15) $(x - 8)(x - 8) =$

$x^2 - 16x + 64$

16) $(2x - 9)(x + 5) =$

$x^2 - 4x - 45$

17) $(2x - 3)(x + 4) =$

$2x^2 + 5x - 12$

18) $(2x + 4)(x + 2) =$

$2x^2 + 8x + 8$

19) $(2x + 2)(x + 3) =$

$2x^2 + 8x + 6$

20) $(2x - 4)(2x + 2) =$

$4x^2 - 4x - 8$

Factoring Trinomials

✎ *Factor each trinomial.*

1) $x^2 + 3x - 10 =$

_____

2) $x^2 + 6x + 8 =$

_____

3) $x^2 - 6x + 8 =$

_____

4) $x^2 - 10x + 16 =$

_____

5) $x^2 - 13x + 40 =$

_____

6) $x^2 + 8x + 12 =$

_____

7) $x^2 - 6x - 27 =$

_____

8) $x^2 - 14x + 48 =$

_____

9) $x^2 + 15x + 56 =$

_____

10) $x^2 - 5x - 36 =$

_____

11) $x^2 + 12x + 36 =$

_____

12) $x^2 + 16x + 63 =$

_____

13) $x^2 + x - 72 =$

_____

14) $x^2 + 18x + 81 =$

_____

15) $x^2 - 16x + 64 =$

_____

16) $x^2 - 18x + 81 =$

_____

17) $2x^2 + 8x + 6 =$

_____

18) $2x^2 + 6x - 8 =$

_____

19) $2x^2 + 12x + 10 =$

_____

20) $4x^2 + 6x - 28 =$

_____

Find more at bit.ly/38EpdJA

Factoring Trinomials - Answers

✎ *Factor each trinomial.*

1) $x^2 + 3x - 10 =$

$(x - 2)(x + 5)$

2) $x^2 + 6x + 8 =$

$(x + 4)(x + 2)$

3) $x^2 - 6x + 8 =$

$(x - 2)(x - 4)$

4) $x^2 - 10x + 16 =$

$(x - 8)(x - 2)$

5) $x^2 - 13x + 40 =$

$(x - 8)(x - 5)$

6) $x^2 + 8x + 12 =$

$(x + 6)(x + 2)$

7) $x^2 - 6x - 27 =$

$(x - 9)(x + 3)$

8) $x^2 - 14x + 48 =$

$(x - 8)(x - 6)$

9) $x^2 + 15x + 56 =$

$(x + 8)(x + 7)$

10) $x^2 - 5x - 36 =$

$(x - 9)(x + 4)$

11) $x^2 + 12x + 36 =$

$(x + 6)(x + 6)$

12) $x^2 + 16x + 63 =$

$(x + 7)(x + 9)$

13) $x^2 + x - 72 =$

$(x - 8)(x + 9)$

14) $x^2 + 18x + 81 =$

$(x + 9)(x + 9)$

15) $x^2 - 16x + 64 =$

$(x - 8)(x - 8)$

16) $x^2 - 18x + 81 =$

$(x - 9)(x - 9)$

17) $2x^2 + 8x + 6 =$

$(2x + 2)(x + 3)$

18) $2x^2 + 6x - 8 =$

$(2x - 2)(x + 4)$

19) $2x^2 + 12x + 10 =$

$(2x + 2)(x + 5)$

20) $4x^2 + 6x - 28 =$

$(2x - 4)(2x + 7)$

The Pythagorean Theorem

✍️ *Do the following lengths form a right triangle?*

1) _____

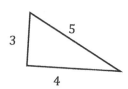

2) _____

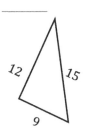

3) _____

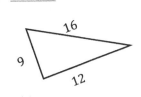

4) _____

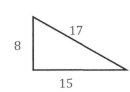

5) _____

6) _____

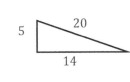

7) _____

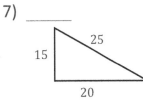

8) _____

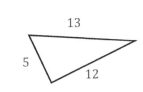

✍️ *Find the missing side.*

9) _____

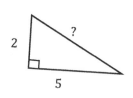

10) _____

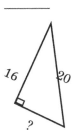

11) _____

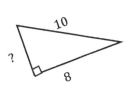

12) _____

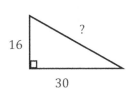

13) _____

14) _____

15) _____

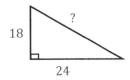

16) _____

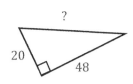

bit.ly/37Jl08v

Find more at

The Pythagorean Theorem - Answers

 Do the following lengths form a right triangle?

1) yes

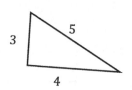

2) yes

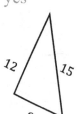

3) no

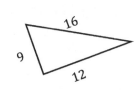

4) yes

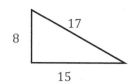

5) no

6) no

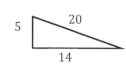

7) yes

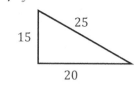

8) yes

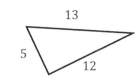

 Find the missing side.

9) 51

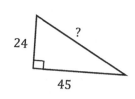

10) 12

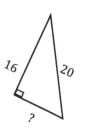

11) 6

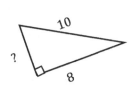

12) 34

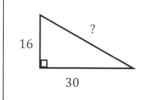

13) 26

14) 13

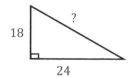

15) 30

16) 52

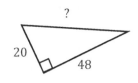

Triangles

✏️ *Find the measure of the unknown angle in each triangle.*

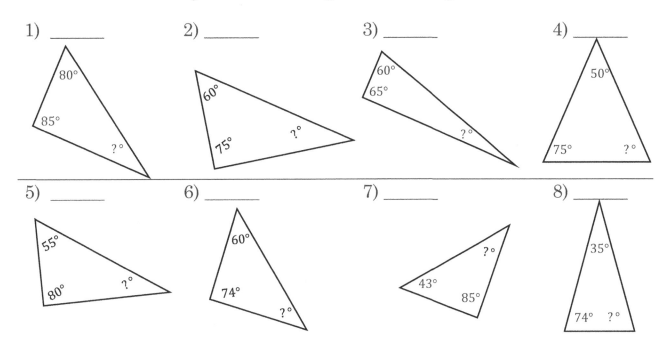

1) _____
80°
85°
?°

2) _____
60°
75°
?°

3) _____
60°
65°
?°

4) _____
50°
75°
?°

5) _____
55°
80°
?°

6) _____
60°
74°
?°

7) _____
?°
43°
85°

8) _____
35°
74° ?°

✏️ *Find area of each triangle.*

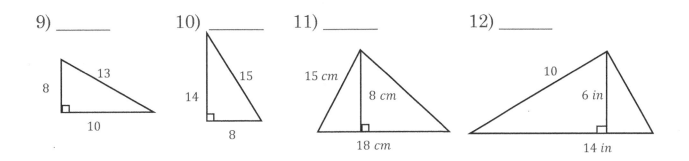

9) _____
13
8
10

10) _____
15
14
8

11) _____
15 cm
8 cm
18 cm

12) _____
10
6 in
14 in

bit.ly/3haZrRg
Find more at

Triangles - Answers

 Find the measure of the unknown angle in each triangle.

1) 15°

80°
85°
?°

2) 45°
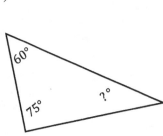

60°
75°
?°

3) 55°
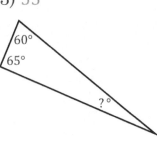

60°
65°
?°

4) 55°
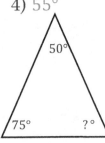

50°
75°
?°

5) 45°
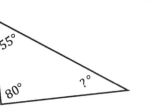

55°
80°
?°

6) 46°
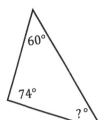

60°
74°
?°

7) 52°
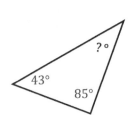

?°
43°
85°

8) 71°
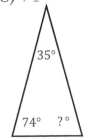

35°
74°   ?°

Find area of each triangle.

9) 40
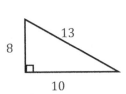

13
8
10

10) 56
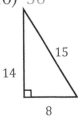

15
14
8

11) 72 cm²
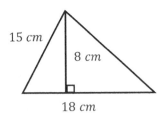

15 cm
8 cm
18 cm

12) 42 in²
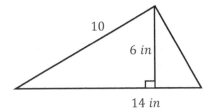

10
6 in
14 in

bit.ly/3haZrRg
Find more at

Polygons

✎ *Find the perimeter of each shape.*

1) (square) _____   2) _____   3) _____   4) (square)
                                                              _____

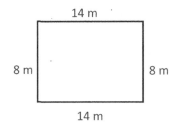

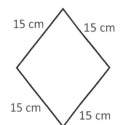

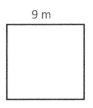

5) *(regular hexagon*   6) _____   7) *(parallelogram*   8) *(regular*
_____   _____   *hexagon)*
                                                                 _____

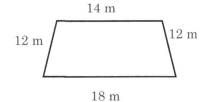

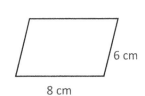

9) _____   10) _____   11) _____   12) *(regular*
                                                            hexagon) _____

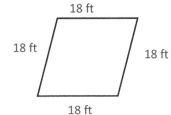

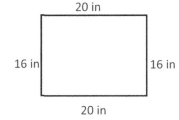

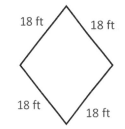

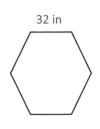

bit.ly/3nFNiGi
Find more at

Polygons - Answers

✍ *Find the perimeter of each shape.*

1) (square) 20 cm

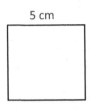

5 cm

2) 44 m

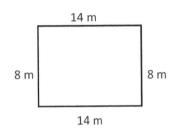

14 m
8 m   8 m
14 m

3) 60 cm

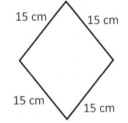

15 cm   15 cm

15 cm   15 cm

4) (square) 36 m

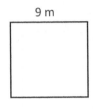

9 m

5) (regular hexagon) 96 m

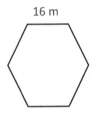

16 m

6) 56 m

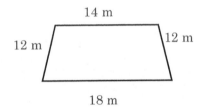

14 m
12 m   12 m
18 m

7) (parallelogram 28 cm

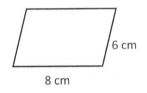

6 cm
8 cm

8) (regular hexagon) 120 ft

20 ft

9) 72 ft

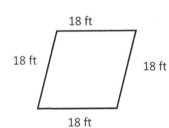

18 ft
18 ft   18 ft
18 ft

10) 72 in

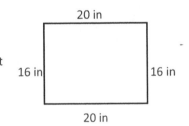

20 in
16 in   16 in
20 in

11) 88 ft

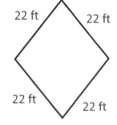

22 ft   22 ft

22 ft   22 ft

12) (regular hexagon) 192 in

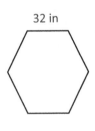

32 in

bit.ly/3nFNiGi
Find more at

Circles

🖋 **Find the Circumference of each circle.** (π = 3.14)

1) ___	2) ___	3) ___	4) ___	5) ___	6) ___

7 in   12 cm   14 ft   13 m   18 cm   15 miles

7) ___	8) ___	9) ___	10) ___	11) ___	12) ___

     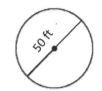

19 in   22 ft   25 m   28 cm   35 miles   50 ft

🖋 **Complete the table below.** (π = 3.14)

	Radius	Diameter	Circumference	Area
Circle 1	2 inches	4 inches	12.56 inches	12.56 square inches
Circle 2		8 meters		
Circle 3				113.04 square ft
Circle 4			50.24 miles	
Circle 5		9 km		
Circle 6	7 cm			
Circle 7		10 feet		
Circle 8				615.44 square meters
Circle 9			81.64 inches	
Circle 10	12 feet			

bit.ly/3nJdOP2

Find more at

Circles - Answers

✍ *Find the Circumference of each circle.* (π = 3.14)

1) 43.96 *in*   2) 75.36 *cm*   3) 87.92 *ft*   4) 81.64 *m*   5) 113.04 *cm*   6)
                                                                          94.2 *miles*

7) 119.32 *in*   8) 138.16 *ft*   9) 157 *m*   10) 175.84 *m*   11) 219.8 *in*   12) 314 *ft*

	Radius	Diameter	Circumference	Area
Circle 1	2 inches	4 inches	12.56 inches	12.56 square inches
Circle 2	4 meters	8 meters	25.12 meters	50.24 square meters
Circle 3	6 ft	12 ft	37.68	113.04 square ft
Circle 4	8 miles	16 miles	50.24 miles	200.96 square miles
Circle 5	4.5 km	9 km	28.26 km	63.585 square km
Circle 6	7 cm	14 cm	43.96 cm	153.86 square cm
Circle 7	5 feet	10 feet	31.4 feet	78.5 square feet
Circle 8	14 m	28 m	87.92 m	615.44 square meters
Circle 9	13 in	26 in	81.64 inches	530.66 square inches
Circle 10	12 feet	24 feet	75.36 feet	452.16 square feet

bit.ly/3nJdOP2

Find more at

Cubes

✎ *Find the volume of each cube.*

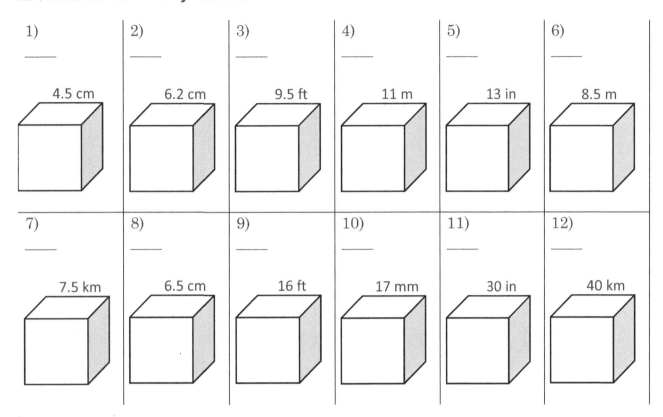

1) _____ 4.5 cm

2) _____ 6.2 cm

3) _____ 9.5 ft

4) _____ 11 m

5) _____ 13 in

6) _____ 8.5 m

7) _____ 7.5 km

8) _____ 6.5 cm

9) _____ 16 ft

10) _____ 17 mm

11) _____ 30 in

12) _____ 40 km

✎ *Find the surface area of each cube.*

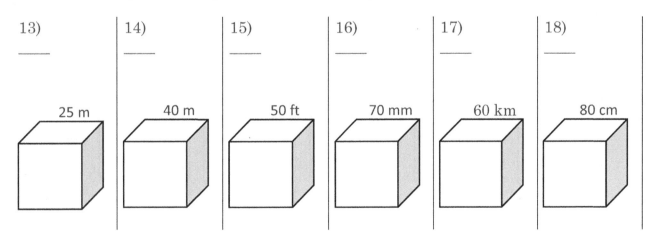

13) _____ 25 m

14) _____ 40 m

15) _____ 50 ft

16) _____ 70 mm

17) _____ 60 km

18) _____ 80 cm

Find more at bit.ly/2M6PfOl

Cubes - Answers

✏️ *Find the volume of each cube.*

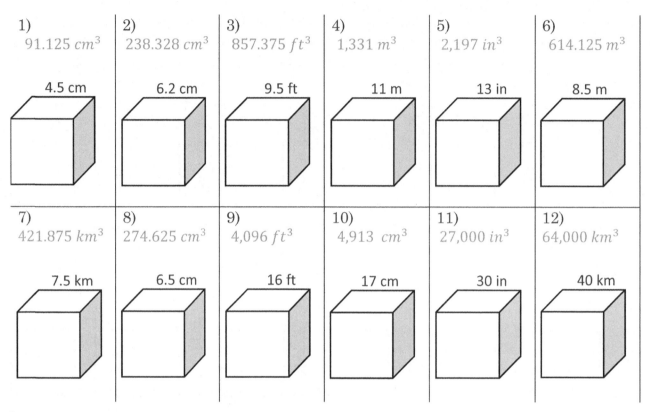

1)
91.125 cm^3

2)
238.328 cm^3

3)
857.375 ft^3

4)
1,331 m^3

5)
2,197 in^3

6)
614.125 m^3

4.5 cm   6.2 cm   9.5 ft   11 m   13 in   8.5 m

7)
421.875 km^3

8)
274.625 cm^3

9)
4,096 ft^3

10)
4,913 cm^3

11)
27,000 in^3

12)
64,000 km^3

7.5 km   6.5 cm   16 ft   17 cm   30 in   40 km

✏️ *Find the surface area of each cube.*

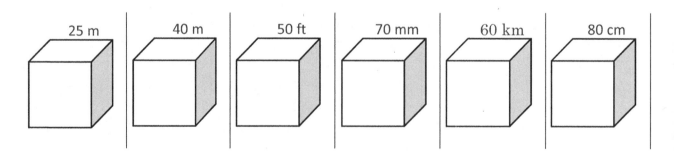

13)
3,750 m^2

14)
9,600 m^2

15)
15,000 ft^2

16)
29,400 mm^2

17)
21,600 km^2

18)
38,400 cm^2

25 m   40 m   50 ft   70 mm   60 km   80 cm

Trapezoids

✎ *Find the area of each trapezoid.*

1) _____

10 cm

8 cm

16 cm

2) _____

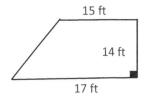

14 m

10 m

18 m

3) _____

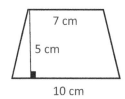

15 ft

14 ft

17 ft

4) _____

7 cm

5 cm

10 cm

5) _____

4 cm

6 cm

12 cm

6) _____

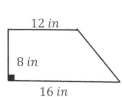

12 in

8 in

16 in

7) _____

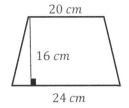

20 cm

16 cm

24 cm

8) _____

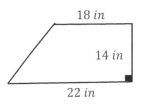

18 in

14 in

22 in

✎ *Solve.*

9) A trapezoid has an area of 80 cm^2 and its height is 8 cm and one base is 12 cm. What is the other base length? _____

10) If a trapezoid has an area of 120 ft^2 and the lengths of the bases are 14 ft and 16 ft, find the height. _____

11) If a trapezoid has an area of 160 m^2 and its height is 10 m and one base is 14 m, find the other base length. _____

12) The area of a trapezoid is 504 ft^2 and its height is 24 ft. If one base of the trapezoid is 14 ft, what is the other base length? _____

bit.ly/3hpKACJ

Find more at

Trapezoids - Answers

✏️ **Find the area of each trapezoid.**

1) $104 \ cm^2$

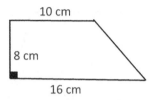

2) $160 \ m^2$

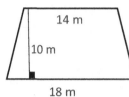

3) $224 \ ft^2$

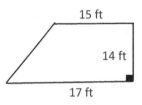

4) $324 \ cm^2$

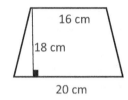

5) $288 \ cm^2$

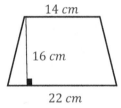

6) $414 \ in^2$

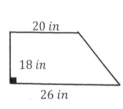

7) $448 \ cm^2$

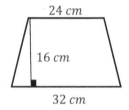

8) $528 \ in^2$

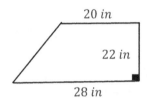

✏️ **Solve.**

9) A trapezoid has an area of 80 cm^2 and its height is 8 cm and one base is 12 cm. What is the other base length? $8 \ cm$

10) If a trapezoid has an area of 120 ft^2 and the lengths of the bases are 14ft and 16ft, find the height. $8 \ ft$

11) If a trapezoid has an area of 160 m^2 and its height is 10 m and one base is 14 m, find the other base length. $18 \ m$

12) The area of a trapezoid is 504 ft^2 and its height is 24 ft. If one base of the trapezoid is 14 ft, what is the other base length? $28 \ ft$

bit.ly/3hpKACJ

Find more at

EffortlessMath.com

Rectangular Prisms

✍ *Find the volume of each Rectangular Prism.*

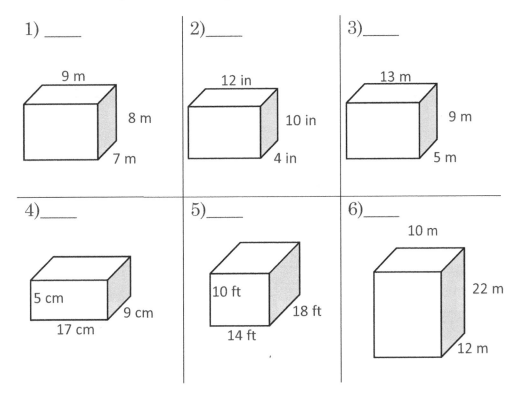

1) ____   9 m, 8 m, 7 m

2) ____   12 in, 10 in, 4 in

3) ____   13 m, 9 m, 5 m

4) ____   5 cm, 17 cm, 9 cm

5) ____   10 ft, 14 ft, 18 ft

6) ____   10 m, 22 m, 12 m

✍ *Find the surface area of each Rectangular Prism.*

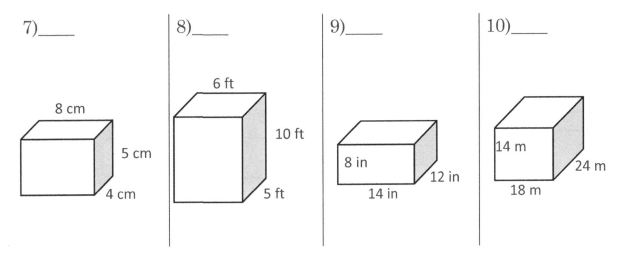

7) ____   8 cm, 5 cm, 4 cm

8) ____   6 ft, 10 ft, 5 ft

9) ____   8 in, 14 in, 12 in

10) ____   14 m, 18 m, 24 m

bit.ly/3nKm2GT

Find more at

Rectangular Prisms - Answers

✍️ *Find the volume of each Rectangular Prism.*

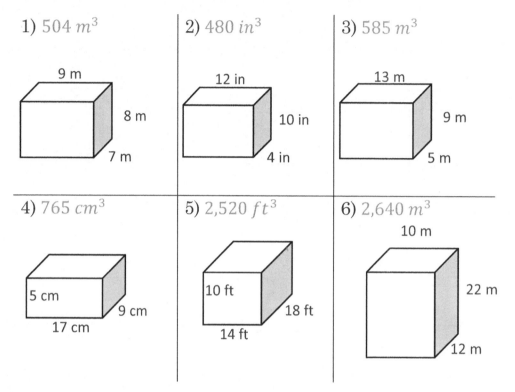

1) $504\ m^3$

2) $480\ in^3$

3) $585\ m^3$

4) $765\ cm^3$

5) $2,520\ ft^3$

6) $2,640\ m^3$

✍️ *Find the surface area of each Rectangular Prism.*

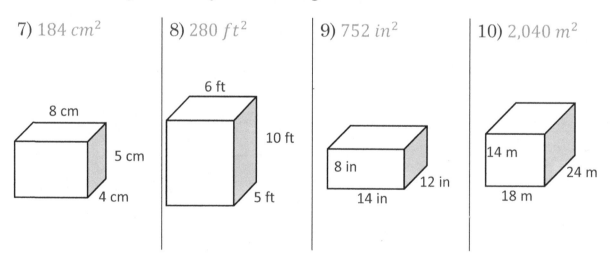

7) $184\ cm^2$

8) $280\ ft^2$

9) $752\ in^2$

10) $2,040\ m^2$

bit.ly/3nKm2GT

Find more at

Cylinder

✏️ *Find the volume of each Cylinder.* ($\pi = 3.14$)

1) _____
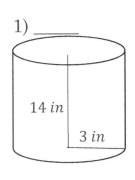
14 in
3 in

2) _____
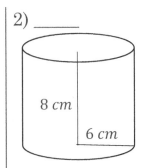
8 cm
6 cm

3) _____
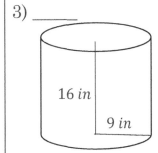
16 in
9 in

4) _____
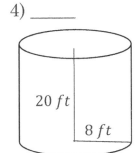
20 ft
8 ft

5) _____
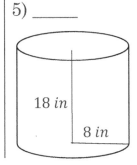
18 in
8 in

6) _____
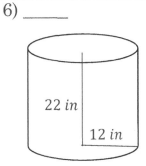
22 in
12 in

✏️ *Find the surface area of each Cylinder.* ($\pi = 3.14$)

7) _____
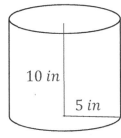
10 in
5 in

8) _____
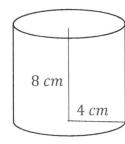
8 cm
4 cm

9) _____
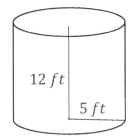
12 ft
5 ft

10) _____
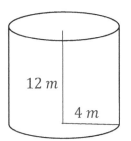
12 m
4 m

bit.ly/37LtcVM
Find more at

Cylinder - Answers

Find the volume of each Cylinder. ($\pi = 3.14$)

1) $395.64 \ in^3$

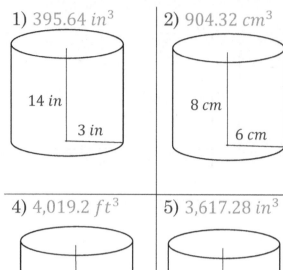

14 in

3 in

2) $904.32 \ cm^3$

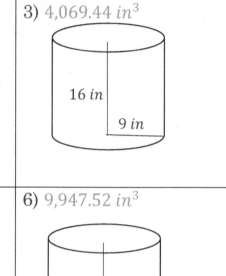

8 cm

6 cm

3) $4,069.44 \ in^3$

16 in

9 in

4) $4,019.2 \ ft^3$

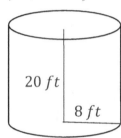

20 ft

8 ft

5) $3,617.28 \ in^3$

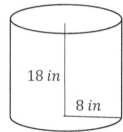

18 in

8 in

6) $9,947.52 \ in^3$

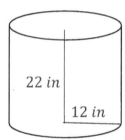

22 in

12 in

Find the surface area of each Cylinder. ($\pi = 3.14$)

7) $471 \ in^2$

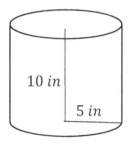

10 in

5 in

8) $301.44 \ cm^2$

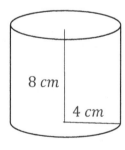

8 cm

4 cm

9) $533.8 \ ft^2$

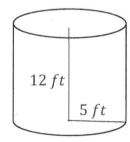

12 ft

5 ft

10) $401.92 \ m^2$

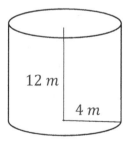

12 m

4 m

bit.ly/37LtcVM

Find more at

EffortlessMath.com

Mean, Median, Mode, and Range of the Given Data

✎ *Find the values of the Given Data.*

1) $6, 12, 1, 1, 5$

Mode: _____   Range: _____

Mean: _____   Median: _____

2) $5, 8, 3, 7, 4, 3$

Mode: _____   Range: _____

Mean: _____   Median: _____

3) $12, 5, 8, 7, 8$

Mode: _____   Range: _____

Mean: _____   Median: _____

4) $8, 4, 10, 7, 3, 4$

Mode: _____   Range: _____

Mean: _____   Median: _____

5) $9, 7, 10, 5, 7, 4, 14$

Mode: _____   Range: _____

Mean: _____   Median: _____

6) $8, 1, 6, 6, 9, 2, 17$

Mode: _____   Range: _____

Mean: _____   Median: _____

7) $12, 6, 1, 7, 9, 7, 8, 14$

Mode: _____   Range: _____

Mean: _____   Median: _____

8) $10, 14, 5, 4, 11, 6, 13$

Mode: _____   Range: _____

Mean: _____   Median: _____

9) $16, 15, 15, 16, 13, 14, 23$

Mode: _____   Range: _____

Mean: _____   Median: _____

10) $16, 15, 12, 8, 4, 9, 8, 16$

Mode: _____   Range: _____

Mean: _____   Median: _____

bit.ly/2KO86gg

Find more at

Mean, Median, Mode, and Range of the Given Data - Answers

✍ *Find the values of the Given Data.*

1) 6, 12, 1, 1, 5

Mode: 1   Range: 11

Mean: 5   Median: 5

2) 5, 8, 3, 7, 4, 3

Mode: 3   Range: 5

Mean: 5   Median: 4.5

3) 12, 5, 8, 7, 8

Mode: 8   Range: 7

Mean: 8   Median: 8

4) 8, 4, 10, 7, 3, 4

Mode: 4   Range: 7

Mean: 6   Median: 5.5

5) 9, 7, 10, 5, 7, 4, 14

Mode: 7   Range: 10

Mean: 8   Median: 7

6) 8, 1, 6, 6, 9, 2, 17

Mode: 6   Range: 16

Mean: 7   Median: 6

7) 12, 6, 1, 7, 9, 7, 8, 14

Mode: 7   Range: 13

Mean: 8   Median: 7.5

8) 10, 14, 5, 4, 11, 6, 13

Mode: *no mode* Range: 10

Mean: 9   Median: 10

9) 16, 15, 15, 16, 13, 14, 23

Mode: 15 *and* 16 Range: 10

Mean: 16   Median: 15

10) 16, 15, 12, 8, 4, 9, 8, 16

Mode: 8 *and* 16 Range: 12

Mean: 11   Median: 10.5

 bit.ly/2KO86gg

Find more at

EffortlessMath.com

Pie Graph

✍ *The circle graph below shows all Wilson's expenses for last month. Wilson spent $200 on his bills last month.*

Answer following questions based on the Pie graph.

Wilson's last month expenses

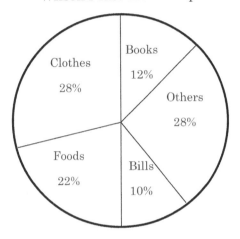

1) How much was Wilson's total expenses last month? __2000_____

2) How much did Wilson spend on his clothes last month? _____

3) How much did Wilson spend for foods last month? _____

4) How much did Wilson spend on his books last month? _____

5) What fraction is Wilson's expenses for his bills and clothes out of his total

   expenses last month? _____

bit.ly/34ECTDv
Find more at

Pie Graph - Answers

✍ *The circle graph below shows all Wilson's expenses for last month. Wilson spent $200 on his bills last month.*

Answer following questions based on the Pie graph.

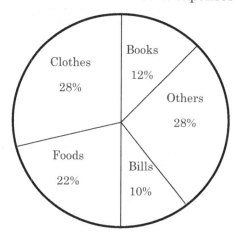

Wilson's last month expenses

1) How much was Wilson's total expenses last month? $2,000

2) How much did Wilson spend on his clothes last month? $560

3) How much did Wilson spend for foods last month? $440

4) How much did Wilson spend on his books last month? $240

5) What fraction is Wilson's expenses for his bills and clothes out of his total expenses last month? $\frac{19}{50}$

Probability Problems

1) If there are 10 red balls and 20 blue balls in a basket, what is the probability that Oliver will pick out a red ball from the basket? _____

Gender	Under 45	45 or older	total
Male	12	6	18
Female	5	7	12
Total	17	13	30

2) The table above shows the distribution of age and gender for 30 employees in a company. If one employee is selected at random, what is the probability that the employee selected be either a female under age 45 or a male age 45 or older? _____

3) A number is chosen at random from 1 to 18. Find the probability of not selecting a composite number. (A composite number is a number that is divisible by itself, 1 and at least one other whole number) _____

4) There are 6 blue marbles, 8 red marbles, and 5 yellow marbles in a box. If Ava randomly selects a marble from the box, what is the probability of selecting a red or yellow marble? _____

5) A bag contains 19 balls: three green, five black, eight blue, a brown, a red and one white. If 18 balls are removed from the bag at random, what is the probability that a brown ball has been removed? _____

6) There are only red and blue marbles in a box. The probability of choosing a red marble in the box at random is one fourth. If there are 132 blue marbles, how many marbles are in the box? _____

Probability Problems - Answers

1) If there are 10 red balls and 20 blue balls in a basket, what is the probability that Oliver will pick out a red ball from the basket? $\frac{1}{3}$

Gender	Under 45	45 or older	total
Male	12	6	18
Female	5	7	12
Total	17	13	30

2) The table above shows the distribution of age and gender for 30 employees in a company. If one employee is selected at random, what is the probability that the employee selected be either a female under age 45 or a male age 45 or older? $\frac{11}{30}$

3) A number is chosen at random from 1 to 18. Find the probability of not selecting a composite number. (A composite number is a number that is divisible by itself, 1 and at least one other whole number) $\frac{7}{18}$

4) There are 6 blue marbles, 8 red marbles, and 5 yellow marbles in a box. If Ava randomly selects a marble from the box, what is the probability of selecting a red or yellow marble? $\frac{13}{19}$

5) A bag contains 19 balls: three green, five black, eight blue, a brown, a red and one white. If 18 balls are removed from the bag at random, what is the probability that a brown ball has been removed? $\frac{18}{19}$

6) There are only red and blue marbles in a box. The probability of choosing a red marble in the box at random is one fourth. If there are 132 blue marbles, how many marbles are in the box? 176

Permutations and Combinations

✍️ *Calculate the value of each.*

1) $5! =$ _____

2) $6! =$ _____

3) $8! =$ _____

4) $5! + 6! =$ _____

5) $8! + 3! =$ _____

6) $6! + 7! =$ _____

7) $8! + 4! =$ _____

8) $9! - 3! =$ _____

✍️ *Solve each word problems.*

9) Sophia is baking cookies. She uses milk, flour and eggs. How many different orders of ingredients can she try? _____

10) William is planning for his vacation. He wants to go to restaurant, watch a movie, go to the beach, and play basketball. How many different ways of ordering are there for him? _____

11) How many 7-digit numbers can be named using the digits 1, 2, 3, 4, 5, 6 and 7 without repetition? _____

12) In how many ways can 9 boys be arranged in a straight line? _____

13) In how many ways can 10 athletes be arranged in a straight line? _____

14) A professor is going to arrange her 7 students in a straight line. In how many ways can she do this? _____

15) How many code symbols can be formed with the letters for the word BLACK? _____

16) In how many ways a team of 7 basketball players can choose a captain and co-captain? _____

bit.ly/34BQgUY

Find more at

Permutations and Combinations - Answers

✎ *Calculate the value of each.*

1) $5! = 120$

2) $6! = 720$

3) $8! = 40,320$

4) $5! + 6! = 840$

5) $8! + 3! = 40,326$

6) $6! + 7! = 5,760$

7) $8! + 4! = 40,344$

8) $9! - 3! = 362,874$

✎ *Solve each word problems.*

9) Sophia is baking cookies. She uses milk, flour and eggs. How many different orders of ingredients can she try? 6

10) William is planning for his vacation. He wants to go to restaurant, watch a movie, go to the beach, and play basketball. How many different ways of ordering are there for him? 24

11) How many 7-digit numbers can be named using the digits 1, 2, 3, 4, 5, 6 and 7 without repetition? 5,040

12) In how many ways can 9 boys be arranged in a straight line? 362,880

13) In how many ways can 10 athletes be arranged in a straight line? 3,628,800

14) A professor is going to arrange her 7 students in a straight line. In how many ways can she do this? 5,040

15) How many code symbols can be formed with the letters for the word BLACK? 120

16) In how many ways a team of 7 basketball players can choose a captain and co-captain? 42

bit.ly/34BQgUY

Find more at

EffortlessMath.com

Function Notation and Evaluation

✎ *Evaluate each function.*

1) $f(x) = x - 1$, find $f(-1)$

_____

2) $g(x) = x + 3$, find $g(4)$

_____

3) $h(x) = x + 9$, find $h(3)$

_____

4) $f(x) = -x - 6$, find $f(5)$

_____

5) $f(x) = 2x - 7$, find $f(-1)$

_____

6) $w(x) = -2 - 4x$, find $w(5)$

_____

7) $g(n) = 6n - 3$, find $g(-2)$

_____

8) $h(x) = -8x + 12$, find $h(3)$

_____

9) $k(n) = 14 - 3n$, find $k(3)$

_____

10) $g(x) = 4x - 4$, find $g(-2)$

_____

11) $k(n) = 8n - 7$, find $k(4)$

_____

12) $w(n) = -2n + 14$, find $w(5)$

_____

13) $h(x) = 5x - 18$, find $h(8)$

_____

14) $g(n) = 2n^2 + 2$, find $g(5)$

_____

15) $f(x) = 3x^2 - 13$, find $f(2)$

_____

16) $g(n) = 5n^2 + 7$, find $g(-3)$

_____

17) $h(n) = 5n^2 - 10$, find $h(4)$

_____

18) $g(x) = -3x^2 - 6x$, find $g(2)$

_____

19) $k(n) = 3n^3 + 2n$, find $k(-5)$

_____

20) $f(x) = -4x + 12$, find $f(2x)$

_____

21) $k(a) = 6a + 5$, find $k(a - 1)$

_____

22) $h(x) = 9x + 3$, find $h(5x)$

_____

bit.ly/3mIs7lF
Find more at

Function Notation and Evaluation - Answers

✎ *Evaluate each function.*

1) $f(x) = x - 1$, find $f(-1)$

-2

2) $g(x) = x + 3$, find $g(4)$

7

3) $h(x) = x + 9$, find $h(3)$

12

4) $f(x) = -x - 6$, find $f(5)$

-11

5) $f(x) = 2x - 7$, find $f(-1)$

-9

6) $w(x) = -2 - 4x$, find $w(5)$

-22

7) $g(n) = 6n - 3$, find $g(-2)$

-15

8) $h(x) = -8x + 12$, find $h(3)$

-12

9) $k(n) = 14 - 3n$, find $k(3)$

5

10) $g(x) = 4x - 4$, find $g(-2)$

-12

11) $k(n) = 8n - 7$, find $k(4)$

25

12) $w(n) = -2n + 14$, find $w(5)$

4

13) $h(x) = 5x - 18$, find $h(8)$

22

14) $g(n) = 2n^2 + 2$, find $g(5)$

52

15) $f(x) = 3x^2 - 13$, find $f(2)$

-1

16) $g(n) = 5n^2 + 7$, find $g(-3)$

52

17) $h(n) = 5n^2 - 10$, find $h(4)$

70

18) $g(x) = -3x^2 - 6x$, find $g(2)$

-24

19) $k(n) = 3n^3 + 2n$, find $k(-5)$

-385

20) $f(x) = -4x + 12$, find $f(2x)$

$-8x + 12$

21) $k(a) = 6a + 5$, find $k(a - 1)$

$6a - 1$

22) $h(x) = 9x + 3$, find $h(5x)$

$45x + 3$

Adding and Subtracting Functions

✍ *Perform the indicated operation.*

1) $f(x) = x + 6$
   $g(x) = 3x + 3$
   Find $(f - g)(2)$

   _____

2) $g(x) = x - 3$
   $f(x) = -x - 4$
   Find $(g - f)(-2)$

   _____

3) $h(t) = 5t + 4$
   $g(t) = 2t + 2$
   Find $(h + g)(-1)$

   _____

4) $g(a) = 3a - 5$
   $f(a) = a^2 + 6$
   Find $(g + f)(3)$

   _____

5) $g(x) = 4x - 5$
   $h(x) = 6x^2 + 5$
   Find $(g - h)(-2)$

   _____

6) $h(x) = x^2 + 3$
   $g(x) = -4x + 1$
   Find $(h + g)(4)$

   _____

7) $f(x) = -2x - 8$
   $g(x) = x^2 + 2$
   Find $(f - g)(6)$

   _____

8) $h(n) = -4n^2 + 9$
   $g(n) = 5n + 6$
   Find $(h - g)(5)$

   _____

9) $g(x) = 3x^2 - 2x - 1$
   $f(x) = 5x + 12$
   Find $(g - f)(a)$

   _____

10) $g(t) = -5t - 8$
    $f(t) = -t^2 + 2t + 12$
    Find $(g + f)(x)$

    _____

bit.ly/3hdeFVO

Find more at

Adding and Subtracting Functions - Answers

✎ *Perform the indicated operation.*

1) $f(x) = x + 6$
   $g(x) = 3x + 3$
   Find $(f - g)(2)$
   -1

2) $g(x) = x - 3$
   $f(x) = -x - 4$
   Find $(g - f)(-2)$
   -3

3) $h(t) = 5t + 4$
   $g(t) = 2t + 2$
   Find $(h + g)(-1)$
   -1

4) $g(a) = 3a - 5$
   $f(a) = a^2 + 6$
   Find $(g + f)(3)$
   19

5) $g(x) = 4x - 5$
   $h(x) = 6x^2 + 5$
   Find $(g - h)(-2)$
   -42

6) $h(x) = x^2 + 3$
   $g(x) = -4x + 1$
   Find $(h + g)(4)$
   4

7) $f(x) = -2x - 8$
   $g(x) = x^2 + 2$
   Find $(f - g)(6)$
   -58

8) $h(n) = -4n^2 + 9$
   $g(n) = 5n + 6$
   Find $(h - g)(5)$
   -122

9) $g(x) = 3x^2 - 2x - 1$
   $f(x) = 5x + 12$
   Find $(g - f)(a)$
   $3a^2 - 7a - 13$

10) $g(t) = -5t - 8$
    $f(t) = -t^2 + 2t + 12$
    Find $(g + f)(x)$
    $-x^2 - 3x + 4$

bit.ly/3hdeFVO
Find more at

Multiplying and Dividing Functions

✍ *Perform the indicated operation.*

1) $g(x) = x + 2$
   $f(x) = x + 3$
   Find $(g.f)(4)$

   _____

2) $f(x) = 2x$
   $h(x) = -x + 6$
   Find $(f.h)(-2)$

   _____

3) $g(a) = a + 2$
   $h(a) = 2a - 3$
   Find $(g.h)(5)$

   _____

4) $f(x) = 2x + 4$
   $h(x) = 4x - 2$
   Find $(\frac{f}{h})(2)$

   _____

5) $f(x) = a^2 - 2$
   $g(x) = -4 + 3a$
   Find $(\frac{f}{g})(2)$

   _____

6) $g(a) = 4a + 6$
   $f(a) = 2a - 8$
   Find $(\frac{g}{f})(3)$

   _____

7) $g(t) = t^2 + 4$
   $h(t) = 2t - 4$
   Find $(g.h)(-3)$

   _____

8) $g(x) = x^2 + 2x + 5$
   $h(x) = 2x + 3$
   Find $(g.h)(2)$

   _____

9) $g(a) = 2a^2 - 4a + 2$
   $f(a) = 2a^3 - 2$
   Find $(\frac{g}{f})(4)$

   _____

10) $g(x) = -4x^2 + 5 - 2x$
    $f(x) = x^2 - 2$
    Find $(g.f)(3)$

    _____

Find more at bit.ly/3ph7kHA

Multiplying and Dividing Functions - Answers

✎ *Perform the indicated operation.*

1) $g(x) = x + 2$

    $f(x) = x + 3$

    Find $(g.f)(4)$

    42

2) $f(x) = 2x$

    $h(x) = -x + 6$

    Find $(f.h)(-2)$

    -32

3) $g(a) = a + 2$

    $h(a) = 2a - 3$

    Find $(g.h)(5)$

    49

4) $f(x) = 2x + 4$

    $h(x) = 4x - 2$

    Find $(\frac{f}{h})(2)$

    $\frac{4}{3}$

5) $f(x) = a^2 - 2$

    $g(x) = -4 + 3a$

    Find $(\frac{f}{g})(2)$

    1

6) $g(a) = 4a + 6$

    $f(a) = 2a - 8$

    Find $(\frac{g}{f})(3)$

    -9

7) $g(t) = t^2 + 4$

    $h(t) = 2t - 4$

    Find $(g.h)(-3)$

    -130

8) $g(x) = x^2 + 2x + 5$

    $h(x) = 2x + 3$

    Find $(g.h)(2)$

    91

9) $g(a) = 2a^2 - 4a + 2$

    $f(a) = 2a^3 - 2$

    Find $(\frac{g}{f})(4)$

    $\frac{1}{7}$

10) $g(x) = -4x^2 + 5 - 2x$

    $f(x) = x^2 - 2$

    Find $(g.f)(3)$

    -259

Composition of Functions

✏️ *Using $f(x) = x + 4$ and $g(x) = 2x$, find:*

1) $f\big(g(1)\big) = $ ____

2) $f\big(g(-1)\big) = $ ____

3) $g\big(f(-2)\big) = $ ____

4) $g\big(f(2)\big) = $ ____

5) $f\big(g(2)\big) = $ ____

6) $g\big(f(3)\big) = $ ____

✏️ *Using $f(x) = 2x + 5$ and $g(x) = x - 2$, find:*

7) $g\big(f(2)\big) = $ ____

8) $g\big(f(-2)\big) = $ ____

9) $f\big(g(5)\big) = $ ____

10) $f\big(f(4)\big) = $ ____

11) $g\big(f(3)\big) = $ ____

12) $g\big(f(-3)\big) = $ ____

✏️ *Using $f(x) = 4x - 2$ and $g(x) = x - 5$, find:*

13) $g\big(f(-2)\big) = $ ____

14) $f\big(f(4)\big) = $ ____

15) $f\big(g(5)\big) = $ ____

16) $f\big(f(3)\big) = $ ____

17) $g\big(f(-3)\big) = $ ____

18) $g\big(g(6)\big) = $ ____

✏️ *Using $f(x) = 5x + 3$ and $g(x) = 2x - 5$, find:*

19) $f\big(g(-4)\big) = $ ____

20) $g\big(f(6)\big) = $ ____

21) $f\big(g(5)\big) = $ ____

22) $f\big(f(3)\big) = $ ____

bit.ly/2WHBkAg

Find more at

Composition of Functions - Answers

✏️ **Using $f(x) = x + 4$ and $g(x) = 2x$, find:**

1) $f\big(g(1)\big) = 6$

2) $f\big(g(-1)\big) = 2$

3) $g\big(f(-2)\big) = 4$

4) $g\big(f(2)\big) = 12$

5) $f\big(g(2)\big) = 8$

6) $g\big(f(3)\big) = 14$

✏️ **Using $f(x) = 2x + 5$ and $g(x) = x - 2$, find:**

7) $g\big(f(2)\big) = 7$

8) $g\big(f(-2)\big) = -1$

9) $f\big(g(5)\big) = 11$

10) $f\big(f(4)\big) = 31$

11) $g\big(f(3)\big) = 9$

12) $g\big(f(-3)\big) = -3$

✏️ **Using $f(x) = 4x - 2$ and $g(x) = x - 5$, find:**

13) $g\big(f(-2)\big) = -15$

14) $f\big(f(4)\big) = 54$

15) $f\big(g(5)\big) = -2$

16) $f\big(f(3)\big) = 38$

17) $g\big(f(-3)\big) = -19$

18) $g\big(g(6)\big) = -4$

✏️ **Using $f(x) = 5x + 3$ and $g(x) = 2x - 5$, find:**

19) $f\big(g(-4)\big) = -62$

20) $g\big(f(6)\big) = 61$

21) $f\big(g(5)\big) = 28$

22) $f\big(f(3)\big) = 93$

PERT Math

Practice Tests

Time to refine your skill with a practice examination

In this section, there are five complete PERT Mathematics Tests. Take these tests to simulate the test day experience. After you've finished, score your test using the answer key.

Before You Start

- You'll need a pencil, a timer, and a four-function calculator to take the test.
- Use the answer sheet provided to record your answers. (You can cut it out or photocopy it)
- For each question there are four possible answers. Choose which one is best.
- After you've finished the test, review the answer key to see where you went wrong and what areas you need to improve.

Good luck!

PERT Mathematics

Practice Test 1

2022

30 questions

Total time for this section: No time limit

You may use a calculator on this Test

1) In the xy −plane, the point $(1, 2)$ and $(−1, 6)$ are on line A. Which of the following points could also be on line A?

   A. $(−3, 2)$

   B. $(−3, 5)$

   C. $(−2, 5)$

   D. $(3, −2)$

2) Four one – foot rulers can be split among how many users to leave each with $\frac{1}{3}$ of a ruler?

   A. 4

   B. 6

   C. 12

   D. 24

3) The set of possible values of n is $\{5, 3, 7\}$. What is the set of possible values of m if $2m = n + 5$?

   A. $\{2, 4, 7\}$

   B. $\{5, 4, 6\}$

   C. $\{3, 2, 5\}$

   D. $\{4, 5, 8\}$

4) Solve for x: $7x + 3 − 2(2x + 1) = 13$

   A. $x = 4$

   B. $x = 6$

   C. $x = −2$

   D. $x = −5$

5) If $x = 25$, then which of the following equations are correct?

   A. $x + 10 = 40$

   B. $4x = 100$

   C. $3x = 70$

   D. $\frac{x}{2} = 12$

6) Jack scored a mean of 80 per test in his first 4 tests. In his 5th test, he scored 90. What was Jack's mean score for the 5 tests?

A. 70

B. 75

C. 80

D. 82

7) The volume of a cube is less than $64\ m^3$. Which of the following can be the cube's side?

A. $\{2, 4, 7\}$

B. $\{5, 4, 6\}$

C. $\{3, 2, 5\}$

D. $\{4, 5, 8\}$

8) Simplify the expression. $(5x^3 - 8x^2 + 2x^4) - (4x^2 - 2x^4 + 2x^3)$

A. $8x^4 + 7x^3 - 8x^2$

B. $5x^4 + x^3 - 9x^2$

C. $4x^4 + 3x^3 - 12x^2$

D. $5x^4 + 2x^3 - 8x^2$

9) If $a = 120°$ and $b = 98°$, what is the value of the c?(Figure not drawn to scale.)

A. $19°$

B. $22°$

C. $35°$

D. $45°$

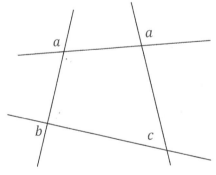

10) The following table represents the value of x and function $f(x)$. Which of the following could be the equation of the function $f(x)$?

A. $f(x) = x^2 - 5$

B. $f(x) = x^2 - 1$

C. $f(x) = \sqrt{x + 2}$

D. $f(x) = \sqrt{x} + 4$

x	$f(x)$
1	5
4	6
9	7
16	8

11) What is the area of an isosceles right triangle that has one leg that measures $6\ cm$?

A. $6\ cm^2$

B. $12\ cm^2$

C. $18\ cm^2$

D. $36\ cm^2$

12) If $0.00104 = \dfrac{104}{x}$, what is the value of x?

A. $1,000$

B. $10,000$

C. $100,000$

D. $1,000,000$

13) A bag is filled with numbered cards from 1 to 15 and picked on at random. What is the probability that the card picked is number 8?

A. $\dfrac{8}{15}$

B. $\dfrac{7}{15}$

C. $\dfrac{2}{15}$

D. $\dfrac{1}{15}$

14) What is the value of x in the figure below?

A. $32°$

B. $46°$

C. $54°$

D. $63°$

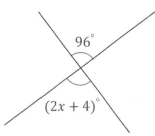

15) What is the value of the following expression? $|-5| + 9 \times 2\frac{1}{3} + (-3)^2 =$

A. 26

B. 35

C. 43

D. 51

16) How many different two-digit numbers can be formed from the digits 6, 7, and 5, if the numbers must be even and no digit can be repeated?

A. 1

B. 2

C. 3

D. 4

17) A rectangular concrete driveway is 25 feet long, 6 feet wide, and 24 inches thick. What is the volume of the concrete?

A. $300 \, ft^3$

B. $660 \, ft^3$

C. $963 \, ft^3$

D. $1,800 \, ft^3$

18) If $\frac{2y}{x} - \frac{y}{3x} = \frac{(\dots)}{3x}$ and $x \neq 0$, what expression is represented by $(\dots)$?

A. $2y + 4$

B. $3y - 6$

C. $5y$

D. $6y$

19) If $360\,kg$ of vegetables is packed in 90 boxes, how much vegetables will each box contain?

   A. $2.5\,kg$

   B. $3\,kg$

   C. $4\,kg$

   D. $6.5\,kg$

20) Each number in a sequence is 4 more than twice the number that comes just before it. If 84 is a number in the sequence, what number comes just before it?

   A. 26

   B. 35

   C. 40

   D. 52

21) 38 is What percent of 50?

   A. 45%

   B. 52%

   C. 64%

   D. 76%

22) A rectangle has $14\,cm$ wide and $5\,cm$ length. What is the perimeter of this rectangle?

   A. $38\,cm$

   B. $43\,cm$

   C. $49\,cm$

   D. $58\,cm$

23) What is the product of all possible values of x in the following equation?

$$|x - 10| = 3$$

   A. 7

   B. 13

   C. 80

   D. 91

24) What is the value of the following expression? $3\frac{1}{4} + 2\frac{4}{16} + 1\frac{3}{8} + 5\frac{1}{2}$

    A. $3\frac{10}{14}$

    B. $4\frac{1}{2}$

    C. $12\frac{4}{16}$

    D. $12\frac{3}{8}$

25) A certain insect has a mass of 85 milligrams. What is the insect's mass in grams?

    A. 0.08

    B. 0.085

    C. 0.85

    D. 85

26) If $m = 6$ and $n = -3$, what is the value of $\frac{5-9(3+n)}{3m-5(2-n)} = ?$

    A. $-\frac{4}{7}$

    B. $-\frac{5}{7}$

    C. $\frac{3}{7}$

    D. $\frac{2}{7}$

27) Clara has 28 cookies. She is inviting 7 friends to a party. How many cookies will each friends get?

    A. 2

    B. 4

    C. 7

    D. 8

28) How long will it take to receive $360 in investment of $240 at the rate of 10% simple interest?

A. 9 years

B. 15 years

C. 18 years

D. 21 years

29) How many hours are there in 1,800 minutes?

A. 20 hours

B. 25 hours

C. 30 hours

D. 33 hours

30) A shoes originally priced at $45.00 was on sale for 15% off. Nick received a 20% employee discount applied to the sale price. How much did Nick pay for the shoes?

A. $30.60

B. $34.50

C. $37.30

D. $42.25

IF YOU FINISH BEFORE TIME IS CALLED, YOU MAY CHECK YOUR WORK ON THIS TEST.   STOP

PERT Mathematics

Practice Test 2

2022

30 questions

Total time for this section: No time limit

You may use a calculator on this Test

1) In a scale diagram, 0.15 inch represents 150 feet. How many inches represent 2.5 feet?

   A. 0.001 *in*

   B. 0.012 *in*

   C. 0.0025 *in*

   D. 0.002 *in*

2) If $\frac{3}{7}$ of Z is 54, what is $\frac{2}{5}$ of Z?

   A. 44.2

   B. 46.3

   C. 48.4

   D. 50.4

3) Mary has 8 blue pens, 2 green pens, and 4 black pens. If she picks out one pen randomly, what is the probability that she picks a blue pen?

   A. $\frac{3}{7}$

   B. $\frac{4}{7}$

   C. $\frac{5}{7}$

   D. $\frac{6}{7}$

4) A car travels at a speed of 72 miles per hour. How far will it travel in 8 hours?

   A. miles

   B. miles

   C. miles

   D. miles

5) If Sam spent $60 on sweets and he spent 25% of the selling price for the tip, how much did he spend?

   A. $66

   B. $69

   C. $72

   D. $75

6) Which of the following numbers has factors that include the smallest factor (other than 1) of 95?

A. 28

B. 32

C. 39

D. 45

7) $\dfrac{4^2+3^2+(-5)^2}{(9+10-11)^2} =?$

A. $\dfrac{25}{32}$

B. 56

C. -56

D. $-\dfrac{25}{32}$

8) Angle A and angle B are supplementary. The measure of angle A is 2 times the measure of angle B. What is the measure of angle A in degrees?

A. $100°$

B. $120°$

C. $140°$

D. $160°$

9) $200(3 + 0.01)^2 - 200 =?$

A. 201.55

B. 361.08

C. 702.88

D. 1,612.02

10) If $x = -2$ in the following equation, what is the value of y? $2x + 3 = \dfrac{y+6}{5}$

A. -9

B. -11

C. -13

D. -15

11) Tomas is 6 feet 8.5 inches tall, and Alex is 5 feet 3 inches tall. What is the difference in height, in inches, between Alex and Tomas?

A. 2.5

B. 7.5

C. 12.5

D. 17.5

12) What is the solution to $\frac{0.02}{0.25} = \frac{1.25}{x}$?

A. 0.150

B. 1.156

C. 11.565

D. 15.625

13) The least of 8 consecutive integers is m, and the greatest is n. What is the value of $\frac{m+n}{3}$ in terms of m?

A. $m + 1$

B. $2m + 8$

C. $\frac{2m+7}{3}$

D. $\frac{2m}{7}$

14) In the infinitely repeating decimal below, 1 is the first digit in the repeating pattern. What is the 68th digit? $\frac{1}{7} = 0.\overline{142857}$

A. 1

B. 2

C. 4

D. 7

15) Yesterday Kylie writes 10% of her homework. Today she writes another 18% of the entire homework. What fraction of the homework is left for her to write?

A. $\frac{7}{25}$

B. $\frac{4}{25}$

C. $\frac{18}{25}$

D. $\frac{10}{25}$

16) In a box of blue and yellow pens, the ratio of yellow pens to blue pens is $2:3$. If the box contains 9 blue pens, how many yellow pens are there?

A. 3

B. 4

C. 5

D. 6

17) What decimal is equivalent to $-\frac{6}{9}$?

A. $-0.\overline{5}$

B. $-0.\overline{6}$

C. $-0.\overline{65}$

D. $-0.\overline{7}$

18) How many positive even factors of 68 are greater than 26 and less than 60?

A. 0

B. 1

C. 2

D. 6

19) Simplify: $-11.6 + 6.7 - 2(-15.3)$

A. 19.7

B. 21.7

C. 23.7

D. 25.7

20) The ratio of two sides of a parallelogram is $2:3$. If its perimeter is $40\ cm$, find the length of its sides.

   A.

   B.

   C.

   D.

21) If x can be any integer, what is the greatest possible value of the expression $2 - x^2$?

   A. -1

   B. 0

   C. 3

   D. 2

22) A store has a container of handballs: 6 green, 5 blue, 8 white, and 10 yellow. If one ball is picked from the container at random, what is the probability that it will be green?

   A. $\frac{1}{5}$

   B. $\frac{6}{11}$

   C. $\frac{6}{29}$

   D. $\frac{8}{25}$

23) In the figure below, F is the midpoint of EH. Which segment has length $2y - x$ centimeters?

   A. EF

   B. GH

   C. EG

   D. FH

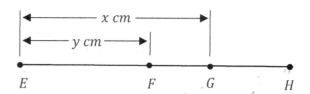

24) 12 Students had a mean score of 75. The remaining 10 students of the class had an average score of 85. What is approximately the mean (average) score of the entire class?

A. 73.5

B. 75.5

C. 77.5

D. 79.5

25) For what value of x is the equation $\frac{x}{4} - 2.5 = 4(6 - 3x) - 2$ true?

A. 0.5

B. 1.8

C. 2

D. 3.4

26) If $x = 3$, what is the approximate value of the following expression? $4x^3 + 2x + \frac{1}{x^2} + 8$

A. 112

B. 115.2

C. 122.1

D. 132.3

27) The probability of drawing a blue candy at random from a bag of 30 candies is $\frac{3}{5}$. After 6 blue candies are removed from the bag, what is the probability of randomly drawing a blue candy from the bag?

A. $\frac{1}{4}$

B. $\frac{1}{2}$

C. $\frac{3}{5}$

D. 1

28) Emma answered 9 out of 45 questions on a test incorrectly. What percentage of the questions did she answer correctly?

   A. 10%

   B. 40%

   C. 68%

   D. 80%

29) $9 - 2(4n + 7) - (5n + 9) =?$

   A. $-30n - 14$

   B. $-13n - 14$

   C. $-25n - 1$

   D. $-31n - 14$

30) If Anna multiplies her age by 5 and then adds 3, she will get a number equal to her mother's age. If x is her mother's age, what is Anna's age in terms of x?

   A. $\frac{x-3}{5}$

   B. $\frac{x-5}{3}$

   C. $3x + 5$

   D. $5x - 3$

IF YOU FINISH BEFORE TIME IS CALLED, YOU MAY CHECK YOUR WORK ON THIS TEST.   STOP

PERT Mathematics Practice Tests

Answer Keys

Now, it's time to review your results to see where you went wrong and what areas you need to improve.

PERT Math Practice Test 1				PERT Math Practice Test 2			
1	D	21	D	1	C	21	D
2	C	22	A	2	D	22	C
3	B	23	D	3	B	23	B
D	A	24	D	4	B	24	D
5	B	25	B	5	D	25	C
6	D	26	B	6	D	26	C
7	A	27	B	7	A	27	B
8	C	28	B	8	B	28	D
9	B	29	C	9	D	29	B
10	D	30	A	10	B	30	A
11	C			11	D		
12	C			12	D		
13	D			13	C		
14	B			14	C		
15	B			15	C		
16	B			16	D		
17	A			17	B		
18	C			18	B		
19	C			19	D		
20	C			20	A		

PERT Mathematics Practice Tests
Answers and Explanations

PERT Mathematics Practice Test 1
Answers and Explanations

1) Choice D is correct

The equation of a line is in the form of $y = mx + b$, where m is the slope of the line and b is the $y-$intercept of the line. Two points $(1,2)$ and $(-1,6)$ are on line A. Therefore, the slope of the line A is: $m = \frac{y_2 - y_1}{x_2 - x_1} = \frac{6-2}{-1-1} = \frac{4}{-2} = -2$

The slope of line A is -2. Thus, the formula of the line A is: $y = -2x + b$, choose a point and plug in the values of x and y in the equation to solve for b. Let's choose point $(1, 2)$. Then:

$$y = -2x + b \rightarrow 2 = -2(1) + b \rightarrow b = 2 + 2 = 4$$

The equation of line A is: $y = -2x + 4$. So, only point $(3, -2)$ could be on the line.

2) Choice C is correct

Divide 4 by $\frac{1}{3}$: $4 \div \frac{1}{3} = 4 \times 3 = 12$

3) Choice B is correct

$2m = n + 5 \rightarrow m = \frac{n+5}{2}$. Substitute each value of n to find the values of m:

$$m = \frac{5+5}{2} = \frac{10}{2} = 5$$

$$m = \frac{3+5}{2} = \frac{8}{2} = 4$$

$$m = \frac{7+5}{2} = \frac{12}{2} = 6$$

The set of m is {5,4,6}

4) Choice A is correct

Apply the distributive property; multiply the -2 by $2x$ and 1.

Then combine like terms:

$$7x + 3 - 2(2x + 1) = 13 \rightarrow 7x + 3 - 4x - 2 = 13 \rightarrow 3x + 1 = 13 \rightarrow 3x = 12$$

Divide both sides of the equation by 3: $x = 4$

5) Choice B is correct

Plug in 25 for x in the equation.

A. $x + 10 = 40 \rightarrow 25 + 10 \neq 40$

B. $4x = 100 \rightarrow 4(25) = 100$

C. $3x = 70 \rightarrow 3(25) \neq 70$

D. $\frac{x}{2} = 12 \rightarrow \frac{25}{2} \neq 12$

Only choice B is correct.

6) Choice D is correct

Jack scored a mean of 80 per test. In the first 4 tests, the sum of scores is: $80 \times 4 = 320$. Now, calculate the mean over the 5 tests: $\frac{320+90}{5} = \frac{410}{5} = 82$

7) Choice A is correct

Volume of the cube is less than $64 \ m^3$. Use the formula of volume of cubes.

Volume $= (one \ side)^3 \Rightarrow 64 = (one \ side)^3$. Find the cube root of both sides.

$64 = (one \ side)^3 \rightarrow one \ side = \sqrt[3]{64} = 4$

Then: $4 =$ one side. The side of the cube is less than 4. Only choice A is less than 4.

8) Choice C is correct

Simplify and combine like terms.

$(5x^3 - 8x^2 + 2x^4) - (4x^2 - 2x^4 + 2x^3) \Rightarrow 5x^3 - 8x^2 + 2x^4 - 4x^2 + 2x^4 - 2x^3 \Rightarrow$

$4x^4 + 3x^3 - 12x^2$

9) Choice B is correct

The sum of all the internal angles of a simple polygon is $180(n-2)$ where n is the number of sides, so $180(4 - 2) = 180 \times 2 = 360$. Vertical angles are congruent. Then:

$\rightarrow 360 = 120 + 120 + 98 + c \rightarrow c = 360 - 338 = 22$

10) Choice D is correct

Let's review the choices when $x = 1$

A. $f(x) = x^2 - 5$ if $x = 1 \rightarrow f(1) = (1)^2 - 5 = 1 - 5 = -4 \neq 5$

B. $f(x) = x^2 - 1$ if $x = 1 \rightarrow f(1) = (1)^2 - 1 = 1 - 1 = 0 \neq 5$

C. $f(x) = \sqrt{x + 2}$ if $x = 1 \rightarrow f(1) = \sqrt{1 + 2} = \sqrt{3} \neq 5$

D. $f(x) = \sqrt{x} + 4$ if $x = 1 \rightarrow f(1) = \sqrt{1} + 4 = 5$

Only choice D provides a correct answer.

11) Choice C is correct

First draw an isosceles triangle. Remember that two legs of the triangle are equal.

Let put a for the legs. Then:

$a = 6 \Rightarrow$ Area of the triangle is $= \frac{1}{2}(6 \times 6) = \frac{36}{2} = 18 \, cm^2$

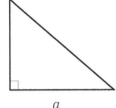

12) Choice C is correct

Solve for x: $0.00104 = \frac{104}{x}$, multiply both sides by x, $(0.00104)(x) = \frac{104}{x}(x)$.

Simplify: $0.00104x = 104$. Divide both side by 0.00104: $\frac{0.00104x}{0.00104} = \frac{104}{0.00104}$, simplify:

$x = \dfrac{104}{0.00104} = 100{,}000$

13) Choice D is correct

The number of cards in the bag is 15. Probability $= \dfrac{number \, of \, desired \, outcomes}{number \, of \, total \, outcomes} = \dfrac{1}{15}$

14) Choice B is correct

$(2x + 4)°$ and $96°$ are vertical angles. Vertical angles are equal in measure. Then:

$2x + 4 = 96 \rightarrow 2x = 92 \rightarrow x = 46°$

15) Choice B is correct

First calculate square of -3: $|-5| + 9 \times 2\frac{1}{3} + 9$

Convert mix number to fraction, then multiply to 9: $|-5| + \frac{63}{3} + 9$

Calculate absolute value and add terms: $5 + 21 + 9 = 35$

16) Choice B is correct

The two-digit numbers must be even, so the only possible two-digit numbers must end in 6, since 6 is the only even digit given in the problem. Since the numbers cannot be repeated, the only possibilities for two-digit even numbers are 76 and 56. Thus, the answer is two possible two-digit numbers.

17) Choice A is correct

First convert 24 inches to feet. 12 inch = 1 feet, thus: $24 \div 12 = 2$ feet. Then, calculate the volume, in cubic feet: $25 \times 6 \times 2 = 300$

18) Choice C is correct

Use properties of equations to determine the missing expression. $\frac{2y}{x} - \frac{y}{3x} = \frac{(\dots)}{3x}$

$\frac{3}{3} \cdot \frac{2y}{x} - \frac{y}{3x} = \frac{(\dots)}{3x} \rightarrow \frac{6y}{3x} - \frac{y}{3x} = \frac{(\dots)}{3x} \rightarrow \frac{6y - y}{3x} = \frac{(\dots)}{3x} \rightarrow (\dots) = 5y$

19) Choice C is correct

Since 90 boxes contain 360 kg vegetable. Therefore, 1 box contains $\frac{360\,kg}{90} = 4\,kg$ vegetable.

20) Choice C is correct

Let n represent a number in the sequence, and let x represent the number that comes just before n.

$n = 4 + 2x \rightarrow 84 = 4 + 2x \rightarrow 80 = 2x \rightarrow x = 40$

21) Choice D is correct

$\frac{38}{50} = 0.76$, converting 0.76 to percent we have: $0.76 = 76\%$. Then, 38 is 76% of 50.

22) Choice A is correct

Perimeter of rectangle is equal to the sum of all the sides of the rectangle:

Perimeter = $2(14) + 2(5) = 28 + 10 = 38\,cm$

23) Choice D is correct

To solve absolute values equations, write two equations. $x - 10$ could be positive 3, or negative 3. Therefore, $x - 10 = 3 \Rightarrow x = 13$

$x - 10 = -3 \Rightarrow x = 7$. Find the product of the solutions: $7 \times 13 = 91$

24) Choice D is correct

$3\frac{1}{4} + 2\frac{4}{16} + 1\frac{3}{8} + 5\frac{1}{2}$

Convert all the fractions to a common denominator (16):

$3\frac{4}{16} + 2\frac{4}{16} + 1\frac{6}{16} + 5\frac{8}{16} = (3 + 2 + 1 + 5) + \left(\frac{4+4+6+8}{16}\right) = 11 + 1\frac{6}{16} = 12\frac{6}{16} = 12\frac{3}{8}$

25) Choice B is correct

One gram is equal to 1,000 milligrams, or 1 milligram is equal to $\frac{1}{1,000}$ gram

Thus, 85 milligrams $= \frac{85}{1,000} = 0.085$ gram

26) Choice B is correct

Substitute 6 for m and -3 for n:

$\frac{5 - 9(3 + n)}{3m - 5(2 - n)} = \frac{5 - 9(3 + (-3))}{3(6) - 5(2 - (-3))} = \frac{5 - 9(0)}{18 - 5(5)} = \frac{5}{18 - 25} = \frac{5}{-7} = -\frac{5}{7}$

27) Choice B is correct

To answer this question, we need to divide 28 by 7: $\frac{28}{7} = 4$

28) Choice B is correct

Simple interest (y) is calculated by multiplying the initial deposit (p), by the interest rate (r), and time (t). $360 = 240 \times 0.10 \times t \rightarrow 360 = 24t \rightarrow t = \frac{360}{24} = 15$

So, it takes 15 years to get $360 with an investment of $240.

29) Choice C is correct

There are 60 minutes in 1 hours. Divide the number of minutes by the number of minutes in 1 hour: $\frac{1,800}{60} = 30$ hours

30) Choice A is correct

First, find the sale price. 15% of $45.00 is $6.75, so the sale price is $45.00 − $6.75 = $38.25. Next, find the price after Nick's employee discount. 20% × $38.25 = $7.65, so, the final price of the shoes is $38.25 − $7.65 = $30.60.

PERT Mathematics Practice Test 2

Answers and Explanations

1) Choice C is correct

Let x be the number of inches representing 2.5 feet.

Set up a proportion and solve for x: $\frac{x}{2.5} = \frac{0.15}{150} \to x = \frac{0.15 \times 2.5}{150} \to x = 0.0025 \ in$

2) Choice D is correct

Set an equation: $\frac{3}{7}Z = 54$

Solve for Z: $\to Z = 54 \times \frac{7}{3} = 126$, then, calculate $\frac{2}{5}Z$: $\frac{2}{5} \times 126 = 50.4$

3) Choice B is correct

The number of pens is 14. The probability of picking a blue pen is: $\frac{8}{14} = \frac{4}{7}$

4) Choice B is correct

To answer this question, multiply 72 miles per hour to $8 \to 72 \times 8 = 576$ miles

5) Choice D is correct

The spent amount is $60, and the tip is 25%. Then: $tip = 0.25 \times 60 = \$15$
Final price = Selling price + tip $\to$ final price $= \$60 + \$15 = \$75$

6) Choice D is correct

To find the smallest factor of 95, list the factors: $1, 5, 19,$ and 95. The smallest factor (other than 1) is 5. Of the choices listed $(28, 32, 39,$ and $45)$, only 45 is a multiple of 5.

7) Choice A is correct

Adding exponents is done by calculating each exponent first and then adding and dividing:

$$\frac{4^2 + 3^2 + (-5)^2}{(9 + 10 - 11)^2} = \frac{16 + 9 + 25}{(8)^2} = \frac{50}{64} = \frac{25}{32}$$

8) Choice B is correct

Angle A and angle B are supplementary, so the sum of their angles is $180°$.

Let a equal the measure of angle A, and let b equal the measure of angle B.

$a + b = 180$

The measure of angle A is 2 times the measure of angle B.

$$a = 2b \rightarrow 2b + b = 180 \rightarrow 3b = 180 \rightarrow b = \frac{180}{3} = 60$$

$$a = 2b = 2(60) = 120$$

Therefore, the measure of angle A is 120°.

9) Choice D is correct

First calculate exponents value, then multiplying and subtracting:

$$200(3 + 0.01)^2 - 200 = 200(3.01)^2 - 200 = 200(9.06) - 200 = 1,612.02$$

10) Choice B is correct

Substitute -2 for x in the equation: $2(-2) + 3 = \frac{y+6}{5} \rightarrow -1 = \frac{y+6}{5} \rightarrow y + 6 = -5 \rightarrow$

$$y = -5 - 6 = -11$$

11) Choice D is correct

First, convert their heights from feet and inches to inches, by multiplying the number of feet by 12 and adding the inches. Tomas: 6 feet $+8.5$ inches. $6(12$ inches$) +8.5$ inches$= 72$ inches $+8.5$ inches $= 80.5$ inches. Alex: 5 feet $+3$ inches. $5(12$ inches$)+3$ inches $= 60$ inches$+3$ inches $= 63$ inches

Then, subtract Alex's height from Tomas's height: $80.5 - 63 = 17.5$

12) Choice D is correct

To eliminate the decimals in this equation, multiply the numerators and denominators by 100:

$$\left(\frac{0.02}{0.25}\right)\left(\frac{100}{100}\right) = \left(\frac{1.25}{x}\right)\left(\frac{100}{100}\right) \rightarrow \left(\frac{2}{25}\right) = \frac{125}{100x} \rightarrow x = \left(\frac{125}{100}\right)\left(\frac{25}{2}\right) = 15.625$$

13) Choice C is correct

The first integer is m, so the second is $m + 1$, the rest are $m + 2, m + 3, m + 4, m + 5, m + 6$ and finally $m + 7$. Since n is the eight and greatest of the integers, $n = m + 7$.

Substitute $m + 7$ for n and simplify: $\frac{m+n}{3} = \frac{m+m+7}{3} = \frac{2m+7}{3}$

14) Choice C is correct

There are 6 digits in the repeating decimal (0.142857), so digit 1 would be the first, seventh, thirteenth digit and so on. To find the 68th digit, divide 68 by 6.

$$68 \div 6 = 11r2$$

Since the remainder is 2, that means the 68ᵗʰ digit is the same as the 2ᵉᵈ digit, which is 4.

15) Choice C is correct

So far, Kylie has written $10\% + 18\% = 28\%$ of the entire homework. That means she has $100\% - 28\% = 72\%$ left to write. $72\% = \frac{72}{100} = \frac{18}{25}$

16) Choice D is correct

Let x be the number of yellow pens. Write a proportion and solve: $\frac{yellow}{blue} = \frac{2}{3} = \frac{x}{9}$

Solve the equation: $18 = 3x \rightarrow x = 6$

17) Choice B is correct

To find the decimal equivalent to $-\frac{6}{9}$, divide 6 by 9. Then:

$$-\frac{6}{9} = -0.66666\ldots = -0.\overline{6}$$

18) Choice B is correct

List the factors of $68: 1$ and 68, 2 and 34, 4 and 17. There is one factor greater than 26 and less than 60.

19) Choice D is correct

First multiply 2 and -15.3. Then, calculate the result.

$-11.6 + 6.7 - 2(-15.3) = -11.6 + 6.7 + 30.6 = 25.7$

20) Choice A is correct

Let the lengths of two sides of the parallelogram be $2x\ cm$ and $3x\ cm$ respectively. Then, its perimeter $= 2(2x + 3x) = 10x$

Therefore, $10x = 40 \rightarrow x = 4$

One side $= 2(4) = 8\ cm$ and other side is: $3(4) = 12\ cm$

21) Choice D is correct

To answer this question, assign several positive and negative values to x and determine what the value of the expression will be:

x	-2	-1	0	1	2
$2 - x^2$	-2	1	2	1	-2

So, the maximum value of the expression is 2.

22) Choice C is correct

The total number of handballs in the container is $6 + 5 + 8 + 10 = 29$. Since there are 6 green handballs, the probability of selecting a green handball is $\frac{6}{29}$

23) Choice B is correct

These facts are given: F is the midpoint of EH.

EG has a length of x cm. EF has a length of y cm.

Use the first two facts to determine that E has a length of $2y$ centimeters:

$GH = EH - EG = 2y - x$

24) Choice D is correct

Total score of first 12 students $= 12 \times 75 = 900$

Total score of remaining 10 students $= 10 \times 85 = 850$

Mean score of the whole class $= \frac{900+850}{22} \approx 79.5$

25) Choice C is correct

Apply the distributive property; multiply 4 by 6 and $-3x$:

$\frac{x}{4} - 2.5 = 24 - 12x - 2$. Simplify: $\frac{x}{4} - 2.5 = 22 - 12x$

Apply the additive inverse property; add $12x$ and 2.5 to both sides of the equation:

$\frac{x}{4} + 12x = 24.5$. Get a common denominator: $\frac{x+48x}{4} = 24.5$

Apply the multiplicative inverse property; multiply both sides of the equation by 4:

$49x = 98$. Divide both sides of the equation by 49: $x = \frac{98}{49} = 2$

26) Choice C is correct

Substitute 3 for x:

$4(3^3) + 2(3) + \frac{1}{(3)^2} + 8 = 108 + 6 + \frac{1}{9} + 8 = 122 + \frac{1}{9} = \frac{1,099}{9} \approx 122.1$

27) Choice B is correct

Start with a proportion to determine the total number of blue candies in the bag.

$\frac{3}{5} = \frac{r}{30} \to \frac{3}{5}(30) = r \to r = 18$

There are currently 18 blue candies out of 30 candies in the bag. After 6 blue candies are removed, there would be 12 blue candies left in the bag and 24 total candies.

The probability of randomly drawing a blue candy would then be $\frac{12}{24} = \frac{1}{2}$

28) Choice D is correct

If Emma answered 9 out of 45 questions incorrectly, then she answered 36 questions correctly.

$$\frac{36}{45} \times 100 = 80\%$$

29) Choice B is correct

First multiply 2 by $4n$ and7: $9 - 8n - 14 - 5n - 9$. Then, combine like terms:

$9 - 8n - 14 - 5n - 9 = -13n - 14$

30) Choice A is correct

Let y be Anna's age. Then:

$x-35$

... So Much More Online!

Effortless Math Online PERT Math Center offers a complete study program, including the following:

✓ Step-by-step instructions on how to prepare for the PERT Math test

✓ Numerous PERT Math worksheets to help you measure your math skills

✓ Complete list of PERT Math formulas

✓ Video lessons for PERT Math topics

✓ Full-length PERT Math practice tests

✓ And much more...

No Registration Required.

Visit **EffortlessMath.com/PERT** to find your online PERT Math resources.

Receive the PDF version of this book or get another FREE book!

Thank you for using our Book!

Do you LOVE this book?

Then, you can get the PDF version of this book or another book absolutely FREE!

Please email us at:

info@EffortlessMath.com

for details.

Author's Final Note

I hope you enjoyed reading this book. You've made it through the book! Great job!

First of all, thank you for purchasing this practice book. I know you could have picked any number of books to help you prepare for your PERT Math test, but you picked this book and for that I am extremely grateful.

It took me years to write this workbook for the PERT Math because I wanted to prepare a comprehensive PERT Math workbook to help test takers make the most effective use of their valuable time while preparing for the test.

After teaching and tutoring math courses for over a decade, I've gathered my personal notes and lessons to develop this practice book. It is my greatest hope that the exercises in this book could help you prepare for your test successfully.

If you have any questions, please contact me at reza@effortlessmath.com and I will be glad to assist. Your feedback will help me to greatly improve the quality of my books in the future and make this book even better. Furthermore, I expect that I have made a few minor errors somewhere in this book. If you think this to be the case, please let me know so I can fix the issue as soon as possible.

If you enjoyed this book and found some benefit in reading this, I'd like to hear from you and hope that you could take a quick minute to post a review on the book's Amazon page. To leave your valuable feedback, please visit: amzn.to/3KP9Pg2

Or scan this QR code.

I personally go over every single review, to make sure my books really are reaching out and helping students and test takers. Please help me help PERT Math test takers, by leaving a review!

I wish you all the best in your future success!

Reza Nazari

Math teacher and author

Made in the USA
Monee, IL
09 August 2022

11257246R00109